CHII
LONDON

Nicholson

An Imprint of Bartholomew
A Division of HarperCollins*Publishers*

A Nicholson Guide

© Nicholson 1994

First published 1989
4th edition 1994

Illustrations by Fiona Macpherson
Design by Bob Vickers

London Maps
© Nicholson, generated from the
Bartholomew London Digital Database

London Underground Map by
permission of London Regional Transport
LRT Registered User No 94/1496

Nicholson
HarperCollins*Publishers*
77-85 Fulham Palace Road
Hammersmith
London W6 8JB

Great care has been taken throughout this book
to be accurate, but the publishers cannot accept
responsibility for any errors which appear, or their
consequences.

Printed in Hong Kong

ISBN 0 7028 2715 0

89/4/48

★ Contents

★ Introduction

From river trips to roller rinks, London is full of attractions for children of all ages. Aimed just as much at Londoners setting out to explore the capital as tourists, *Children's London* has hundreds of ideas on things to do and lots of useful information for parents and children out and about in London.

For first-time visitors it covers getting around, traditional ceremonies and events, the main sights and museums, plus chapters on where to eat and shop. Londoners will find it equally invaluable with sections on sports organisations, art, music and theatre workshops, London at work, as well as information on organising birthday parties, holidays and fun days out.

Children's London is very easy to use. Each entry has an address, telephone number, opening times and map reference (at the top right hand side), which refers to the street maps at the back of the book.

This guide will help you discover a huge variety of activities in and around London that the whole family can enjoy.

Generally central London numbers are 071- and Greater London are 081-. From April 1995, the number 1 will be inserted after the 0 in the area code. If you are not sure which to dial, telephone the operator (100 - free).

★ Getting Around

To get around London you have a choice of transport: the familiar red London bus, the speedier tube, the computer-operated Docklands Light Railway and the London taxi.

★ *Buses* ★ ★ ★ ★ ★ ★ ★ ★ ★ ★ ★ ★ ★ ★

The best way to start exploring London is to travel by bus. Sit on the top deck for the best view. Under 14s pay a reduced flat fare until *22.00,* as do 14 and 15 year-olds with a Child Rate Photocard (available from Post Offices, London Transport travel information centres and underground stations). Up to two under-5s per person travel free.

Instead of going on a sightseeing tour, you could travel on one of the bus routes below. They take in a large majority of the city's sights and you will only have to buy a day pass. The names printed in capital letters are terminal points. Refer to the bus map on page 161.

4 WATERLOO, Aldwych, Fleet St, St Paul's, Barbican, Islington, Finsbury Park, ARCHWAY.

11 LIVERPOOL STREET STATION, Bank, St Paul's, Fleet St, Aldwych, Strand, Trafalgar Sq, Whitehall, Westminster, Victoria, Sloane Sq, Chelsea, FULHAM BROADWAY.

14 TOTTENHAM COURT ROAD, Charing Cross Rd, Shaftesbury Ave, Piccadilly, Hyde Park Corner, Knightsbridge, South Kensington, Fulham, PUTNEY.

If you have any enquiries go to one of the travel information centres listed below or phone 071-222 1234 for a *24-hr* travel information service:

Euston Underground Station	**1 F4**
Hammersmith Underground Station	
Heathrow Underground Station	
King's Cross Underground Station	**2 A4**
Liverpool Street Underground Station	**5 F1**
Oxford Circus Underground Station	**4 D2**
Piccadilly Circus Underground Station	**4 E3**
Victoria Underground Station	**7 B2**

15 PADDINGTON, Edgware Rd, Marble Arch, Oxford St, Regent St, Piccadilly Circus, Trafalgar Sq, Strand, Aldwych, Fleet St, St Paul's, Monument, Tower, Aldgate, Stepney, Poplar, EAST HAM.
24 PIMLICO, Victoria, Westminster, Whitehall, Trafalgar Sq, Leicester Sq, Charing Cross Rd, Tottenham Court Rd, Camden Town, HAMPSTEAD.
38 VICTORIA, Hyde Park Corner, Piccadilly, Shaftesbury Ave, Bloomsbury, Islington, Dalston, CLAPTON.

★ *Tube* ★ ★ ★ ★ ★ ★ ★ ★ ★ ★ ★ ★ ★ ★ ★

London's underground railway is known as the tube and was built for fast travel. Transport in the streets is often slow, but below ground tubes have the tunnels to themselves.
There are underground maps in all of the stations. Each line has a name and is clearly indicated in a separate colour; it is sometimes easier to follow the colours than to go by the names of the lines. Also see map on page 176.
Under 14s travel at a reduced fare, as do 14 and 15 year-olds with a Child Rate Photocard (available from Post Offices, London Transport travel information centres and underground stations). Under 5s travel free.

★ *Docklands Light Railway* ★ ★ ★ ★ ★ ★

The Docklands Light Railway (DLR) runs on viaducts throughout the Docklands area, offering excellent views. The trains are computer-operated, although there is a conductor on board to collect tickets.

★ *Concessionary Fares* ★ ★ ★ ★ ★ ★ ★ ★

Buying a *Travelcard* will save you money and time. It can be bought from any London Transport office, travel information centre, British Rail or underground station (not beyond Northwood, Queen's Park or Woodford on the Epping Line). The combined British Rail, underground, Docklands Light Railway and bus network in Greater London is divided into five zones. You just choose which zones you want to travel in and buy the appropriate *Travelcard*. You can then travel on any combination of train, tube and bus within your selected zones, any number of times for the duration of the ticket's validity. The one-day *Travelcard* gives you unlimited off-peak travel for the day; it can only be bought after *09.30*.

Piccadilly Circus

★ *Taxis* ★ ★ ★ ★ ★ ★ ★ ★ ★ ★ ★ ★ ★ ★ ★ ★

London taxis can be hailed in the street if the yellow 'For Hire' or 'Taxi' sign above the windscreen is lit up. Charges vary according to the distance you travel and are recorded on the meter.

★ *Cars* ★ ★ ★ ★ ★ ★ ★ ★ ★ ★ ★ ★ ★ ★ ★ ★

If you are travelling by car, parking in London can be very difficult, especially in the centre of town. Very few attractions have their own car park, so to ease the strain of searching for those elusive unoccupied parking meters we have listed some of the main central London car parks. Most of the car parks are operated by National Car Parks Ltd (071-499 7050) and they are easily spotted by their large yellow NCP signs. Opening hours and prices vary and can be very expensive. Please check with the individual car park.

EC4 St Paul's, Cannon Street, Ludgate Circus
NCP Distaff Lane,   5 D3
Distaff Lane. 071-236 1333.
NW1 Euston, Marylebone, Regent's Park
NCP Dorset House,   1 B6
Marylebone Road. 071-935 6078.
SE1 Waterloo, South Bank Complex, Southwark
NCP Snowfields,   5 E5
Kipling St. 071-407 9779.
SW1 Westminster, Victoria, St James's
NCP Abingdon St. 071-222 8621.   7 E1
NCP Arlington House,   4 D4
Arlington St. 071-499 3312.
NCP Semley Place, Ebury St. 071-730 4282.   7 B2
W1 West End
NCP Park Lane. 071-262 1814.   4 A3
NCP Wardour St. 071-437 5383.   4 E2
W2 Paddington, Bayswater
NCP Arthur Court, Queensway. 071-221 2906.   3 C3
W8 Kensington
NCP Young St. 071-937 7420.   3 C5
WC1 Holborn, Bloomsbury
NCP Adeline Place, YMCA, 3 Great Russell St.
071-637 0964.   4 E1
NCP Selkirk House, Museum St. 071-836 2039.   4 F2
WC2 Leicester Square, Strand
NCP Upper St Martin's Lane. 071-836 7451.   4 F3
NCP Swiss Centre. 071-734 1032.   4 E3

★ *Tourist Information Centres* ★ ★ ★ ★

London Tourist Board Information Centres
Provide travel and tourist information for London and
England. Most languages spoken. Instant hotel reserva-
tions, theatre and tour bookings, sales of guide books,
maps and guides. Also provide a *24-hour* telephone
information service **Visitorcall** (0839 123456). For places
to visit with children (0839 123424), for school holiday
events (0839 123404).
London Tourist Board & Convention Bureau   7 B1
Victoria Station Forecourt SW1. *Open Easter-Oct 08.00-
19.00 Mon-Sun; Nov-Mar 08.00-19.00 Mon-Sat, 08.00-16.00
Sun.*
Heathrow Tourist Information Centre
Heathrow Terminals 1, 2 & 3, Heathrow Airport, Middx.
Open 08.30-18.00 Mon-Sun.

Liverpool Street Tourist Information Centre **5 F1**
Liverpool Street Station EC2. *Open 08.15-19.00 Mon, 08.15-18.00 Tue-Sat, 08.30-16.45 Sun.*

Selfridges Tourist Information Centre **4 B2**
400 Oxford St W1. *Open 09.30-19.00 Mon-Fri (to 20.00 Thur), 09.00-18.00 Sat.*

British Travel Centre **4 E4**
12 Lower Regent St SW1. British Tourist Authority information centre. Personal callers only. *Open 09.00-18.30 Mon-Fri, 10.00-16.00 Sat & Sun; May-Sep 09.00-17.00 Sat.*

City of London Information Centre **5 D2**
St Paul's Churchyard EC4. 071-332 1456. Information and advice with specific reference to the City. *Open May-Sep 09.30-17.00 Mon-Sun; Oct-Apr 09.30-17.00 Mon-Fri, 09.30-12.30 Sat.*

★ *In London with the Under 5s* ★ ★ ★ ★

London can be exhausting with young children, so try not to plan too much for one day. You might find it easier to try a sightseeing trip round the famous landmarks, a tour on a double-decker bus or a river trip to Hampton Court or Kew (see *Trips & Tours* on page 11).

Try to avoid the main commuter hours when public transport is jam-packed – *08.00-09.30 & 16.30-18.30 Mon-Fri.* You will also find it easier to take a folding push-chair or carrying frame with so many escalators, stairs and pavements to contend with, especially during the rush hour.

If you don't have the right equipment, you can hire it from one of the following:

Chelsea Baby Hire
51 Lamberhurst Road SE27. 081-670 7304. Free delivery and collection (central London). Push-chairs, baby carriers, car seats, carrycots etc from one night onwards. Fully qualified nannies available for baby-sitting. Free brochure supplied on request.

Nappy Express
128 High Road, Friern Barnet N11. 081-361 4040. Free delivery and collection service. All the nursery equipment you may need plus nappies, baby goods and household items. Cloth nappy laundry service. You can hire from one afternoon onwards. Member of the Baby Equipment Hirers Association. Free brochure supplied on request.

London is full of restaurants and many offer portions for children under five. These are a sensible bet as they will usually have booster chairs and a welcoming attitude! (See *Eating Out* on page 114).

Entertainment tends to be for older children, but some theatres put on matinées for 3-5 year-olds, especially in the school holidays (see *Entertainment* on page 81).

It is a good idea to ensure that young children unable to speak clearly for themselves, and non-English speaking children, have a note on them of their name and address (or hotel).

Bear in mind that most underground stations do not have public toilets; however, toilets and nursing rooms are located in the following British Rail stations: Euston, King's Cross, Liverpool Street, Paddington, St Pancras, Victoria and Waterloo.

★ Trips & Tours

★ By Coach ★ ★ ★ ★ ★ ★ ★ ★ ★ ★ ★ ★ ★ ★

Sightseeing tours are usually on double-decker buses or coaches with a commentary. Be careful which one you choose; some only take a few hours but others take the whole day. None of the ones listed below are specifically for children – but all would be suitable for 6 year-olds and up. The London Tourist Board Information Centre, Victoria Station Forecourt SW1 sells tickets for a selection of sightseeing tours; alternatively you can telephone the organisations direct to reserve seats.

Big Bus Company
Waterside Way SW17. 081-944 7810. Operates *1½-hour* panoramic tour of the City and the West End. Live commentary.

Docklands Tours
London Docklands Visitor Centre, 3 Limeharbour, Isle of Dogs E14. 071-512 1111. *2-hour* tours of Docklands accompanied by guides from the London Docklands Development Corporation. See restored wharves and warehouses, conservation areas, historic buildings, magnificent waterside views. Audio-visual presentation in Visitor Centre *45 mins prior to departure*. Tours at *14.00 Tue; 10.30 Thur & Sun*. Book in advance.

Evan Evans   **4 E4**
26 Cockspur St SW1. 071-930 2377. Operates a variety of tours; *full-day, morning* or *afternoon* plus a *2½-hour* general drive around the capital and a *30-minute* cruise on the Thames. Also runs extended tours out of London.

Frames Rickards   **1 G5**
11 Herbrand St WC1. 071-837 3111. *Morning* and *afternoon* tours of the City and the West End. Also runs tours out of London.

Golden Tours   **7 B2**
4 Fountain Square, Buckingham Palace Rd SW1. 071-233 7030. Choose from a number of tours including an open-top tour of the City and the West End, a 'hop on hop off' tour

where you can see the sights at your leisure, or a trip to one of London's famous street markets.

Harrods 6 F1

Sightseeing Tours Dept, Lower Ground Banking Hall, Harrods, Knightsbridge SW1. 071-581 3603. Undoubtedly the most luxurious coach tour of London, *2-hour* tours *Mon-Sun, full-day tour Thur only*. Taped commentary in eight languages plus refreshments. Harrods also operates tours to Stratford-upon-Avon *(Sun only)* and Blenheim Palace. Tickets, reservations and information on 071-581 3603.

Original London Sightseeing Tours

London Coaches, Jew's Row SW18. Information: 081-877 1722. Round London tours in traditional double-decker buses, some of which are open-topped.

Star Safari

Half-day tours taking in the lives and lifestyles of the rich and famous with commentary by guides who will give you an insight into London and its glitterati. Tours depart from the Forum Hotel SW7 (**6 C2**), Bressenden Place SW1 (**7 C1**) and Trafalgar Square WC2 (**4 E4**). Details and bookings on (0932) 854721.

★ *By Foot* ★ ★ ★ ★ ★ ★ ★ ★ ★ ★ ★ ★ ★ ★ ★

Citisights of London 5 E4

c/o The Old Operating Theatre Museum, 9a St Thomas St SE1. 071-955 4791. Varied programme of walks specialising in archeological and literary tours. Offers customised walks for special tours.

London Wall Walk 5 D1

Museum of London, London Wall EC2. 071-600 3699. Devised by the Museum of London, this is the best way to see the Roman and medieval city walls. The route takes about *1-2 hours* to complete and in that time you'll cover about 2 miles of London's streets. Buy the booklet *Roman Wall Walk* from the museum shop to set you on the right trail.

The *Original* London Walks

PO Box 1708, NW6 4LW. 071-624 3978. A choice of more than 40 walks all over London including occasional specialised walks for children. Walks last *2 hours* and take place *Mon-Sun*.

Streets of London

16 The Grove N3. 081-346 9255. Guided walking tours with a regular programme of scheduled walks, regardless of weather. Also private tours for clubs, societies, schools etc.

Also see walks section in *Out of Doors* on page 74.

★ *By Helicopter* ★ ★ ★ ★ ★ ★ ★ ★ ★ ★

Alan Mann Helicopters
Fairoaks Airport, Chobham, Surrey. (0276) 857471. A sightseeing flight in a helicopter has to be the ideal way of viewing the capital. Single-engined helicopters will take you up the River Thames for an unforgettable ride, with the pilot as your guide. Maximum of four passengers. Under 8s should be accompanied by an adult.

★ *By Plane* ★ ★ ★ ★ ★ ★ ★ ★ ★ ★ ★

London Flightseeing Tours
081-767 9055. Chauffered ride from home to the airfield at Stapleford, Essex, followed by a *30-min* sightseeing flight over the famous London landmarks. *Phone for details.*

★ *By Private Guide* ★ ★ ★ ★ ★ ★ ★ ★ ★

British Tours   **4 C2**
6 South Molton St W1. 071-629 5267. Wide variety of individual tours throughout London and surrounding areas with qualified driver/guides.

Go-By-Guides Ltd
17 Woodfield, Parkhill Rd NW3. 071-722 7506. Sightseeing tours by private car accompanied by trained driver/guides.

Tour Guides Ltd   **4 B2**
57 Duke St W1. 071-495 5504. A booking bureau for Tourist Board registered tourist guides throughout the UK. Car, coach and walking tours can be arranged for individuals or groups in over 30 languages.

★ *River Trips* ★ ★ ★ ★ ★ ★ ★ ★ ★ ★ ★

One of the best ways of appreciating the city is to take a boat trip. The buildings lining the banks of the River Thames range from run-down warehouses to palaces. You can visit some of London's famous sights by river, such as the Tower of London, Hampton Court, Greenwich and Kew Gardens. During the *summer, daily* services run from the piers listed overleaf, but travellers may board at any of the other piers en route. It is important to note that times vary according to the tides and the weather; it is always advisable to telephone for details first. And remember to check times of return boats at the pier on arrival. The London Tourist Board provides an excellent River Trips information service on (0839) 123432 (recorded information).

DOWNRIVER SERVICES ▰▰▰▰▰▰▰▰

Charing Cross Pier   4 G4
071-839 3572. Trips to the Tower (*20-minute journey*) and Greenwich (*45-minute journey*) Apr-Oct every 30 minutes between 10.30-16.00 Mon-Sun; Nov-Mar every 45 minutes between 10.30-15.00 Mon-Sun.

Greenwich Pier
Return services to Charing Cross Pier (*45-minute journey*), Tower Pier (*30-minute journey*) and Westminster Pier (*45-minute journey*). *Phone the individual piers for details.*

Tower Pier   5 F4
071-488 0344. Trips to Westminster (*20-minute journey*) every 20 minutes 11.00-18.40 in summer (every 40 mins 11.00-17.20 Nov-Mar). Ferry to HMS Belfast (*5-minute journey*) every 15 minutes 11.00-18.00 in summer only.

Westminster Pier   4 F5
071-930 4097. Trips to the Tower (*30-minute journey*) every 20 minutes 10.30-16.00, and to Greenwich (*50-minute journey*) every 30 minutes 10.30-16.00; all year.

UPRIVER SERVICES ▰▰▰▰▰▰▰▰

Westminster Pier   4 F5
Westminster Passenger Services operate boat trips to Putney (*30-minute journey*), Kew (*1½-hour journey*), Richmond (*2-hour journey*), Hampton Court (*3-4-hour journey*) during summer only. Phone 071-930 2062 for departure times.
There are local services to Hampton Court (*Easter-Sep*) from Richmond and Kingston. *Phone 081-546 2434 for details.*

★ *By Canal* ★ ★ ★ ★ ★ ★ ★ ★ ★ ★ ★ ★

Before 1830 there were no long-distance railways in Britain and most roads were very rough. The easiest way to move heavy cargoes was by water, so dozens of canals were cut through the countryside and cities. Early canal boats were pulled by horse. The horse walked beside the canal and towed the boat with a rope. Today there are still some interesting canals in London. You will probably not see any horse-drawn barges, but beside every canal there is still a path, which the horses once used, called a towpath. You can walk along these paths in London for many miles. Here are some ideas for canal trips:

Canal Water Bus   1 D1
London Waterbus Company, Camden Lock Place NW1. 071-

482 2660. Boats run from Little Venice stopping at London Zoo and continuing to Camden Lock or from Camden Lock to Little Venice. *Apr-Oct 10.00-17.00 Mon-Sun every hour on the hour; Nov-Mar 10.30-15.45 Sat & Sun only. Phone for details of departure times.*

Jason's Trip

Opposite 60 Blomfield Rd W9. 071-286 3428. The traditional narrowboat *Jason* leaves Little Venice for *1½-hour* return trip, with commentary, through Regent's Park (with London Zoo) to Camden Lock. Disembark to look round the craft shops if you like, or the market at *weekends*. Refreshments and lunch available. *Phone for details of departure times.*

Jenny Wren Cruises   **1 D1**

250 Camden High St NW1. 071-485 4433. *1½-hour* round trips along Regent's Canal passing London Zoo, Regent's Park and Little Venice, with commentary on the canal and its history. Regular trips from *Feb-Nov Mon-Sat. Phone for details of departure times.*

★ Calendar

For exact days, times and places of special events contact the London Tourist Board's Information Service on 0839 123400 or check the listings in *Time Out*.

★ *January* ★ ★ ★ ★ ★ ★ ★ ★ ★ ★ ★ ★ ★

Chinese New Year Festival   **4 E3**
Gerrard St W1. Papier-mâché dragons, the lion dance and firecrackers bring Chinatown to life. Plus Chinese arts, crafts and food. *Jan or Feb*.

International Boat Show   **6 A3**
Earl's Court Exhibition Centre, Warwick Rd SW5. 071-385 1200. The largest boat show in Europe. *Early Jan*.

The London Parade
One of the largest parades in Europe with some 7000 performers – from marching bands and cheerleaders to colourful floats and veteran vehicles. Starts at *12.00* at Parliament Square (**4 F5**) and ends at Berkeley Square (**4 C3**) passing via Trafalgar Square and Piccadilly.

★ *February* ★ ★ ★ ★ ★ ★ ★ ★ ★ ★ ★ ★

Astronomy Exhibition - ASTROFEST   **3 B5**
Kensington Town Hall, Hornton St W8. 071-915 0054. Displays of telescopes, astronomical clocks and a "starlab". Guest speakers. *Early Feb*.

Daily Express Motor Racing Show   **6 A3**
Earl's Court Exhibition Centre, Warwick Rd SW5. 071-385 1200. A must for motor racing enthusiasts. *Mid Feb*.

Holiday on Ice
Wembley Arena, Wembley, Middx. 081-900 1234. Pantomime on ice.

International Computer Show
Wembley Conference and Exhibition Centre, Empire Way, Wembley, Middx. 081-902 8833. Exhibition of new hardware and software, plus virtual reality simulators. Also held in *Jul*.

The Great Spitalfields Pancake Race   **5 G1**
Brushfield St E1. 071-375 0441. Watch various teams running with frying pans, tossing their pancakes as they go. Starts at *midday*.

★ *March* ★ ★ ★ ★ ★ ★ ★ ★ ★ ★ ★ ★ ★ ★ ★

Daily Mail Ideal Home Exhibition   **6 A3**
Earl's Court Exhibition Centre, Warwick Rd SW5. 071-385 1200. Full of new and interesting gadgets. Very popular and always crowded. *Mid Mar.*

Oranges and Lemons Service   **5 A2**
St Clement Danes, Strand WC2. 071-242 8282. After a special service, oranges and lemons are distributed to children while the traditional tune is played on handbells.

Oxford v Cambridge University Boat Race
River Thames. Putney to Mortlake university boat race over four miles. Watch from the riverbanks or from one of the bridges. Get there early for a good view. *Sat afternoon in Mar or Apr.*

Sailboat
Crystal Palace National Sports Centre SE19. 081-778 0131. Exhibition of dinghies and small sailing boats. *No fixed date.*

Spring Stampex   **7 D2**
Royal Horticultural Society Halls, 80 Vincent Sq SW1. 071-834 4333. National stamp exhibition. Also hold Autumn Stampex. Contact the British Philatelic Centre for details (071-490 1005). *Early Mar.*

★ *April* ★ ★ ★ ★ ★ ★ ★ ★ ★ ★ ★ ★ ★ ★ ★

Butterworth Charity   **5 C1**
St Bartholomew-the-Great, Smithfield EC1. 071-606 5171. Traditionally the presentation of a sixpence to 'poor widows', now the presentation of hot cross buns to children. *Good Fri following 11.30 service.* Open-air service (weather permitting).

Easter Kite Festival
Blackheath SE3. Demonstrations of single line, box, sport and stunt kites. Parachuting teddy bears, kite ballet and "rokkuku" – Japanese-style kite fighting. *Phone 071-836 1666 for details.*

Easter Show   **6 F5**
Battersea Park SW11. Colourful carnival; fairground, side stalls, various stage acts. *Easter Sun.*

London Harness Horse Parade   **1 C4**
Regent's Park NW1. Fine horses and carts, brewers'
vans and drays on parade. Judging starts at *09.45*
followed by a procession twice round the Inner Circle.
Easter Mon.

London Marathon
The famous 26-mile race starting at *09.30* at Greenwich
Park SE10 and finishing at Westminster Bridge SW1 (**4 F5**).
For information contact 071-620 4117. *Late Apr.*

Model Railway Exhibition   **7 D2**
Royal Horticultural Society Halls, 80 Vincent Sq SW1. 071-
834 4333. International collection of model railways including 20 working layouts. *Five days mid Apr.*

Tower of London Church Parade   **5 G3**
Tower of London, Tower Hill EC3. 071-709 0765. Yeomen
Warders in state dress are inspected, and parade before and
after morning service on *Easter Sun, 11.00. Also Whit Sun &
Sun before Xmas.*

★ *May* ★ ★ ★ ★ ★ ★ ★ ★ ★ ★ ★ ★ ★ ★ ★ ★

Chelsea Flower Show   **6 F3**
Chelsea Royal Hospital, Royal Hospital Rd SW3. 071-821
3000. (*24-hr* information line 071-828 1744.) Superb flower
displays. *Three days late May.*

FA Cup Final
Wembley Stadium, Wembley, Middx. 081-900 1234. The
best match of the English football season. *Late Apr/early
May.*

London Dollshouse Festival   **3 B5**
Kensington Town Hall, Hornton St W8. 071-937 5464.
Display of dollshouses plus stalls selling equipment for making your own dollshouse. *Not suitable for very young children. Early May.*

Putney & Hammersmith Amateur Regattas
Rowing regattas make exciting watching from the banks of
the Thames. Contact the Amateur Rowing Association for
information on 081-748 3632. *Late Apr/early May.*

Rugby League Challenge Cup Final
Wembley Stadium, Wembley, Middx. 081-900 1234.
Contact Rugby Football League (0532) 624637. *Late
Apr/early May.*

Rugby Union Cup Final
Twickenham Rugby Football Ground, Whitton Rd,
Twickenham, Middx. 081-892 8161. *Early May.*

★ *June* ★ ★ ★ ★ ★ ★ ★ ★ ★ ★ ★ ★ ★ ★ ★ ★

Beating Retreat   4 F4
Horse Guards Parade SW1. Military display of marching and
drilling bands. Trumpeters, massed bands and pipe and drums.
Some floodlit performances. Phone 071-222 7684 for tickets.

Garter Ceremony
St George's Chapel, Windsor. Service attended by the
Queen, preceded by a colourful procession with the
Household Cavalry and Yeomen of the Guard. Ceremony
dates from the 14th century. *Mon afternoon of Ascot week
(usually third week in Jun).*

Lord's Test Match
Lord's Cricket Ground, St John's Wood Rd SW8. Phone
071-289 1615 for tickets. *Jun or Jul.*

Trooping the Colour
The route is from Buckingham Palace SW1 along the Mall
to Horse Guards Parade, Whitehall and back again.
Pageantry at its best for the Queen's official birthday. *11.00
Sat nearest 11 Jun.* If you want tickets to the event or to
one of the full-scale dress rehearsals apply in writing to
the Brigade Major, Household Division, Horseguards,
Whitehall SW1 between *1 Jan & 1 Mar.* Tickets are award-
ed by ballot.

Wimbledon Lawn Tennis Championships
All England Lawn Tennis & Croquet Club, Church Rd SW19.
081-946 2244. 'Wimbledon Fortnight', the world's most
famous championship. Matches *from 14.00 Mon-Sat. Last
week Jun & first week Jul.*

★ *July* ★ ★ ★ ★ ★ ★ ★ ★ ★ ★ ★ ★ ★ ★ ★

Annual London International Festival of Street   4 D3
Entertainers
A competition taking place around Carnaby Street and
Golden Square W1. Acts change about *every 20 minutes*
with plenty of variety – juggling, clowning, dance, theatre
and mime. Contact 071-287 0907 (Alternative Arts) for further details. *Third weekend Jul.*

Doggett's Coat & Badge Race   5 F4
River Thames, Tower Pier to Chelsea. 071-626 3531.
Sculling race for Thames watermen from London Bridge to
Chelsea. Originated in 1715. *Late Jul.*

National Festival of Music for Youth   5 A4
South Bank Concert Halls SE1. 071-928 3002. Young
musicians perform *throughout Jul.*

Proms (Henry Wood Promenade Concerts)   **3 E5**
Royal Albert Hall, Kensington Gore SW7. 071-589 8212.
Concerts for all classical music fans. *Late Jul until Sep.*
Royal Tournament   **6 A3**
Earl's Court Exhibition Centre, Warwick Rd SW5. 071-385
1200. Impressive military spectacle with marching displays
and massed brass bands. *Two weeks mid Jul.*

★ *August* ★ ★ ★ ★ ★ ★ ★ ★ ★ ★ ★ ★ ★ ★ ★

British Teddy Bear Festival   **3 B5**
Kensington Town Hall, Hornton St W8. 071-937 5464.
Biggest display of teddy bears in the UK. 10,000 antique and
new teddies for sale. *Late Aug.*
Notting Hill Carnival   **3 B4**
Ladbroke Grove and Notting Hill W11. West Indian carnival
with colourful floats, steel bands and dancing in the streets.
Bank holiday Sun & Mon.

★ *September* ★ ★ ★ ★ ★ ★ ★ ★ ★ ★ ★ ★ ★

Election of Lord Mayor of London   **5 D2**
Procession from the church of St Lawrence Jewry,
Gresham St EC2 to the Guildhall EC2. 071-606 3030.
Michaelmas Day, 29 Sep.
Last Night of the Proms   **3 E5**
Royal Albert Hall, Kensington Gore SW7. 071-589 8212.
Now a tradition. Audiences sing along with the orchestra
and wave banners. Tickets by qualification system only. *15
Sep or nearest Sat.*

★ *October* ★ ★ ★ ★ ★ ★ ★ ★ ★ ★ ★ ★ ★ ★ ★

Annual Full Tidal Closure
Thames Barrier Visitor Centre, Unity Way, Eastmoor
St SE18. 081-854 1373. The annual closing of the
Thames Barrier. See the huge barriers lifting out of the
water.
Autumn Stampex   **7 D2**
Royal Horticultural Society Halls, 80 Vincent Sq SW1. See
March.
Children's Book Week
National festival with events taking place at venues all over
the country. Mainly at bookshops and libraries in the London

area. For details phone the information hotline: 081-958 4398. *Second week in Oct.*

Costermonger's Harvest Festival 4 F3
St Martin-in-the-Fields, Trafalgar Sq WC2. 071-930 1862. Service attended by the Pearly Kings and Queens, in their colourful regalia. *15.00, second Sun in Oct.*

Horse of the Year Show
Wembley Arena, Wembley, Middx. 081-900 1234. Fine show-jumping. *Early Oct.*

Punch & Judy Fellowship Festival 4 F3
Covent Garden Piazza WC2. An all-day festival of Punch & Judy in the piazza. *First Sun in Oct from 10.30-17.30.*

Trafalgar Day Service & Parade 4 E4
Trafalgar Sq WC2. Organised by the Navy League to commemorate the death of Lord Nelson with a naval parade and service. *Sun nearest to Trafalgar Day, 21 Oct.*

★ *November* ★ ★ ★ ★ ★ ★ ★ ★ ★ ★ ★ ★ ★

Admission of the Lord Mayor Elect 5 D2
Guildhall, Gresham St EC2. 071-606 3030. The Lord Mayor takes office. Colourful ceremony including handing over of insignia by former Lord Mayor. *Fri before Lord Mayor's Show (second Fri in Nov).*

Christmas Lights 4 D2
Regent St and Oxford St W1. Festive lights to attract Christmas shoppers. Best seen from *16.00* onwards. *Late Nov-6 Jan (Twelfth Night).*

Daily Mail International Ski Show   6 A3
Earl's Court Exhibition Centre, Warwick Rd SW5. 071-385 1200. Holiday kit for the keen skier. *Oct/Nov.*

Guy Fawkes Night
Anniversary of the Gunpowder Plot of 1605. Firework displays and bonfires throughout London and the whole country. *Evening 5 Nov.*

London to Brighton Veteran Car Run   4 B5
Hyde Park Corner W1. Cars leave here for Brighton. Colourful event with some contestants in costume. *08.00 first Sun in Nov.*

Lord Mayor's Procession & Show
The newly elected Lord Mayor is driven in his state coach from the Guildhall (**5 D2**) to the Law Courts (**5 A2**) to be received by the Lord Chief Justice. The biggest ceremonial event in the city. *Second Sat in Nov.*

Remembrance Sunday
Poppies sold in the streets to raise money for ex-service-men. The service to remember the dead of the two world wars is held at the Cenotaph, Whitehall SW1 (**4 F5**), with a salute of guns. *11.00, second Sun in Nov.*

Royal Smithfield Show   6 A3
Earl's Court Exhibition Centre, Warwick Rd SW5. 071-385 1200. Exhibition of agricultural machinery, supplies and services. Also livestock. *Early Dec.*

State Opening of Parliament
The Queen is driven in the Irish state coach from Buckingham Palace (**4 D5**) to the House of Lords (**4 F5**). A royal salute is fired from St James's Park. *Mid Nov.*

★ *December* ★ ★ ★ ★ ★ ★ ★ ★ ★ ★ ★ ★ ★ ★

Carol Services   4 F6
Westminster Abbey, Broad Sanctuary SW1. 071-222 7110. Carol services on *26, 27 & 28 Dec.*

Carol Singing   4 E4
Trafalgar Sq WC2. *Every evening from about 14 Dec.*

Christmas Tree   4 E4
Trafalgar Sq WC2. Norwegian spruce donated each year by the citizens of Oslo. Carol singing round the tree. *Mid Dec-6 Jan (Twelfth Night).*

New Year's Eve   4 E4
Trafalgar Sq WC2. Singing of *Auld Lang Syne* by massed crowds around the fountains.

Tower of London Church Parade   **5 G3**
Tower of London, Tower Hill EC3. See *April*.

★ *Daily Ceremonies* ★ ★ ★ ★ ★ ★ ★ ★ ★

Ceremony of the Keys   **5 G3**
Tower of London, Tower Hill EC3. 071-709 0765. The chief warder of the Yeomen Warders of the Tower locks the West Gates, the Middle Tower and the Byward Tower. One of the oldest continuous military ceremonies in the world. Takes place *21.40 Mon-Sun*. Apply in writing for tickets to the Governor of the Tower, enclosing an sae.

Changing of the Guard   **4 D5**
Buckingham Palace SW1. Takes place inside the palace railings – see the guards on their way from Chelsea or Wellington barracks. Palace ceremony at *11.30 (on alternate days in winter); lasts ½ hour*.

★ Seeing the Sights

London's history began in AD43 when the Romans invaded and succeeded in bridging the Thames. Their take-over was so complete that the area became an important military and administrative base. They built the London Wall to defend the centre, traces of which are still visible today. This was to determine the shape of what we now call the City of London for some 1300 years.

The next major event in London was in the 11th century when William the Conqueror won the Battle of Hastings in 1066. He was responsible for building one of London's most well-known landmarks, the Tower of London. By the turn of the following century London's first mayor, a position held in the 13th century by Dick Whittington, was elected and medieval street markets sprang up in the narrow, cramped lanes of the City (look out for street names like Bread Street and Milk Street). A system of local government was established in the Guildhall in the City and by the middle of the 17th century almost a quarter of a million people lived in the City or its up-market suburb, Westminster. Even the king, Henry VIII, moved from the countryside back into town and built up the palaces at St James's and Whitehall.

In 1666, the Great Fire destroyed three-fifths of the City, flames igniting every wooden building in its path. Out of the ashes grew a massive scheme which was to create the London we know today. Streets were broadened and all the new buildings were made of brick. Christopher Wren masterminded the construction of 51 of the City's churches as well as the massive restoration of St Paul's Cathedral. London quickly expanded well beyond the Roman walls, absorbing numerous surrounding villages in the process which have given their names to different parts of London. London's growth resulted from rising commercial importance (the City is still one of the world's major financial centres), the Industrial Revolution and, more recently, developing public transport which pushed new suburbs well out into the countryside. You can trace London's history in the buildings, monuments, churches and famous houses, all of which have their own story to tell.

> **Children's Discounts**
> While you're sightseeing, take advantage of discounts on admission. Most attractions offer half-price tickets for children under 16.

★ *Bird's Eye Views* ★ ★ ★ ★ ★ ★ ★ ★ ★ ★ ★

Alexandra Palace
Muswell Hill N22. 081-365 2121. Built in 1873, it was partially destroyed in a dramatic fire. Now restored to its former glory, there are excellent views from its 77-metre (250ft) high terrace over north London, Kent, Surrey, Essex and Hertfordshire.

Hampstead Heath NW3
A delightful view of London, as painted by Constable. Particularly good vantage points are the high ground by Jack Straw's Castle, Whitestone Pond and Parliament Hill.

Monument   **5 E3**
Monument St EC3. 071-626 2717. Built by Wren 1671-7 to commemorate the Great Fire of London. It stands 61 metres (202ft) high, one foot in height for every foot in distance from the site of the baker's shop in Pudding Lane where the Great Fire started. You can climb up to the top for a wonderful view of the city, but beware if you're inclined to feel dizzy; there are 311 steps! *Open Apr-Sep 09.00-18.00 Mon-Fri, 14.00-18.00 Sat & Sun; Oct-Mar 09.00-16.00 Mon-Sat. Closed Sun. Last admission 20 minutes before closing time.* Charge.

St Paul's Cathedral   **5 D2**
Ludgate Hill EC4. 071-248 2705. A magnificent view of the City, the Wren churches (there are 50 others), the Tower and London Pool. It is 112 metres (365ft) from the pavement to the cross, with some 627 steps. No mean feat if you make it to the top here. *Open* (for sightseeing) *09.00-16.30 Mon-Sat.* Charge.

Tower Bridge   **5 G4**
071-407 0922. Superb views over London and the Thames from the high walkways when you visit 'The Celebration Story' – the Tower Bridge exhibition. *Open Apr-Oct 10.00-18.30 Mon-Sun; Nov-Mar 10.00-17.15 Mon-Sun. Last admission 45 minutes before closing time. Closed Bank hols.* Charge.

Westminster Cathedral   **7 C1**
Ashley Place SW1. 071-834 7452. The campanile or bell-

tower on the north-west corner is dedicated to Saint Edward the Confessor and stands 83 metres (273ft) high. It has excellent views over Westminster and the Thames and can be reached by lift which is usually *open Apr-Sep 09.00-17.00 Mon-Sun.* Charge.

★ *Buildings in History* ★ ★ ★ ★ ★ ★ ★ ★

Admiralty Arch   4 F4
Entrance to the Mall SW1. A memorial to Queen Victoria, it is now significant as part of the professional route for the Queen to Buckingham Palace.

Albert Memorial   3 E5
Kensington Gore SW7. Queen Victoria selected Sir George Gilbert Scott's design for the memorial to her beloved husband, Prince Albert, in 1872. He died suddenly of typhoid aged only 42. The £120,000 needed to build it was raised from the public and Parliament. Due to extensive restoration work, the memorial is currently covered.

Bank of England   5 E2
Threadneedle St EC2. 071-601 5545. Serves as banker to the government, as well as leading British and international banks, and is commonly known as the 'old lady of Threadneedle Street'. The vaults hold the nation's gold reserves. The outer walls are still the original design by Sir John Soane, architect to the Bank 1788-1833, but were rebuilt by Sir Herbert Baker 1925-39. There is no entry to the public except to the museum (see *Museums & Galleries* on page 48).

Banqueting House   4 F4
Whitehall SW1. 071-930 4179. When James I dreamt of rebuilding his palace, this is as far as he got; a 17th-century building (1619-25) by the famous architect, Inigo Jones, added to the Palace of Whitehall, once the principal residence of the court. Magnificent ceilings painted by Rubens, for which he was given a knighthood. It was from here that Charles I stepped through a window to his execution. *Open 10.00-17.00 Mon-Sat. Last admission 16.30.* Charge.

Barbican Centre   2 E6
Silk St EC2. 071-638 4141. The Barbican Arts Centre is the centre-piece of a large, modern residential scheme, the largest complex of its kind in Western Europe. The original barbican, a fortified medieval watch-tower outside London's wall, gives its name to the development. The Barbican Theatre is the London home of the Royal Shakespeare Company, whilst the Barbican Hall acts similarly for the London Symphony Orchestra. Children's cinema club *every Sat 14.30* (see *Entertainment* on page 83). *Open 10.00-20.00 Mon-Sun.* Charge.

British Telecom Tower 1 E6

Maple St W1. 071-580 6767. Completed in 1964, this 174-metre (580ft) high needle of concrete and glass is one of the tallest buildings in London. It had to be this high to transmit above all the other buildings! Formerly known as the Post Office Tower, it marked the start of a trend to high-rise buildings and was to change London's skyline. *Closed to the public.*

Buckingham Palace 4 D5

St James's Park SW1. The official London residence of the Queen. The royal flag flies from the roof if the Queen is at home. In 1826 the Prince Regent asked John Nash to make the Duke of Buckingham's country house into the palace we know today. The view of the Palace from the Mall is really the 'back door' as the other side of the Palace faces onto a 16-hectare (40-acre) garden. The State Rooms are *open Aug-Oct 09.30-17.30 Mon-Sun. Last admission 16.30.* The Changing of the Guard is a very popular attraction which takes place at *11.30* within the palace railings (*every day in summer, alternate days in winter*). The guards who have been on duty that morning march away and their place is taken by a new group of guardsmen (see *Daily Ceremonies* on page 23). Two other areas you can visit are the Royal Mews and the Queen's Gallery (see *Museums & Galleries* on pages 49 & 53).

Chelsea Royal Hospital 6 G4

Royal Hospital Road SW3. 071-730 0161. This beautiful building by Wren was founded by Charles II as a home for old soldiers. It houses 400 army pensioners, unmistakable in their tricorn hats and frock coats, blue in winter, red in summer. *Open 10.00-12.00 & 14.00-16.30 Mon-Sat, 14.00-16.00 Sun. Closed Sun in winter.* Free.

Chiswick House

Burlington Lane W4. 081-995 0508. Lovely villa built 1725-30 by the 3rd Earl of Burlington, a patron of the arts. The house was designed as a gallery where fine pictures were hung and artists and writers entertained. *Open Apr-Sep 10.00-13.00 & 14.00-18.00 Mon-Sun; Oct-Mar 10.00-13.00 & 14.00-16.00 Wed-Sun.* Charge.

Clarence House 4 D5

Stable Yard Gate SW1. Mansion by Nash 1825 and now the home of Her Majesty the Queen Mother, but has a long list of previous royal inhabitants, such as William IV, Queen Victoria's mother and the present Queen before her accession. Princess Anne, the Princess Royal, was born here. *Closed to the public.*

Cleopatra's Needle   **4 G4**

Victoria Embankment SW1. Has nothing to do with the Egyptian Queen; it is from Helipolis (about 1500 BC) and records the triumphs of the Egyptian king, Rameses the Great. It was presented by the Viceroy of Egypt and set up next to the Thames in 1878. When it was erected a bundle of newspapers, coins, toys, a railway guide, hairpins and a picture of Queen Victoria were buried underneath for posterity.

Cutty Sark

King William Walk, Greenwich Pier SE10. 081-858 3445. Built as a tea clipper in 1869 it is now in dry dock at Greenwich. The name *Cutty Sark* is taken from the poem *Tam O'Shanter* by Robert Burns. You can explore the ship and see where the sailors ate, slept and worked. The galley and cabins all have their own furniture. She stands as a permanent reminder of the days when Britain dominated the world's oceans. Nearby is *Gipsy Moth IV*, the boat in which Sir Francis Chichester sailed single-handed around the world in 1966. Both *open Apr-Sep 10.00-17.00 Mon-Sat, 12.00-17.30 Sun;* Cutty Sark *open Oct-Mar 10.00-16.30 Mon-Sat, 12.00-16.30 Sun.* Charge.

Downing Street   **4 F5**

SW1. Number 10 is the official residence of the Prime Minister. Mrs Thatcher lived here the longest of any Prime

Downing Street

Minister in recent history. Number 11 has been the Chancellor of the Exchequer's home since early last century. Iron gates prevent complete access for the public.

Eltham Palace

Off Court Yard, Eltham SE9. 081-294 2548. The remains of a moated royal palace, originally in the countryside some miles from London or Westminster. The palace was built by the Bishop of Durham and passed to the crown in 1311. Several kings used it as a royal country seat; in fact Henry IV was married here. All that remains of the original palace is the foundations, the Great Hall with its hammerbeam roof and the beautiful 14th-century bridge over the moat. *Open Apr-Sep 10.00-18.00 Thur & Sun; Oct-Mar 10.00-16.00 Thur & Sun.* Free.

Goldsmith's Hall   **5 D2**

Foster Lane EC2. 071-606 7010. The Goldsmith's Company was given the responsibility of maintaining the standard of purity of gold and silver goods. If the items came up to standard they were stamped with a special mark – a leopard's head – to verify their quality. This became known as a hallmark – a mark applied at Goldsmith's Hall. The Goldsmith's Company is one of the oldest and wealthiest City Livery companies and their hall reflects their status – well worth a visit. *Open by appointment only. To arrange tours contact the City of London Information Centre, St Paul's Churchyard EC4, 071-332 1456 for details of dates and times of open days.* Free.

Guildhall   **5 D2**

Off Gresham St EC2. 071-606 3030. The Guildhall, a centre of civic government for over 1000 years, has witnessed trials of traitors, brilliant receptions, presidents and royal personages. It is, of course, at the heart of the City and its customs and it is here in the Great Hall that the Lord Mayor and Sheriffs are elected each year.

The Great Hall occupies the exact site of the building erected in 1411. Gog and Magog will undoubtedly catch your attention. These two giants are supposed to represent the conflict between the British and the Trojan invaders. The hall is now used for ceremonial occasions like the Lord Mayor's banquet. *To arrange tours telephone or write well in advance to the Keeper's Office, PO Box 270, Guildhall EC2P 2EJ, stating preferred dates and times. Tours by arrangement every 2 hours between 10.00 & 16.00 Mon-Sat, except when closed for functions.* Specialist library concerned with the history of London *open 09.30-17.00 Mon-Sat.* The Museum of the Clockmakers Company is contained within the library and is *open 09.30-16.45 Mon-Fri.* Free.

Hampton Court Palace

Hampton Court, East Molesey, Surrey. 081-781 9500. Riverside palace built in 1514 for Cardinal Wolsey, who displeased Henry VIII for not arranging a quick divorce from his first wife, Catherine of Aragon. To please Henry, Cardinal Wolsey presented him with Hampton Court, but unfortunately it didn't do him any good. It was built to be the largest palace in Europe and gives a good idea of what a Tudor royal palace was really like. Henry built the Great Hall where he held huge banquets. He was supposedly so impatient to get it finished his men worked throughout the night by candle light to complete it. In 1689 King William and Queen Mary commissioned Sir Christopher Wren to rebuild parts of the palace. See the sumptuous state rooms painted by Vanbrugh, Verrio and Thornhill and a famous picture gallery full of Italian masterpieces.

In the grounds are an orangery, mellow courtyards, the 'great vine' and the maze to wander round. The formal gardens are probably among the greatest in the world. *Tours at 11.15, 13.45 & 15.15 Mon-Sun. Large groups should phone or write to the Booking Office at the Palace (above address) stating preferred dates and times. Additional tours by arrangement. Open mid Mar-Oct 10.15-18.00 Mon, 09.30-18.00 Tue-Sun; Nov-mid Mar 10.15-16.30 Mon, 09.30-16.30 Tue-Sun.* Charge.

Harrods   6 F1

Knightsbridge SW1. 071-730 1234. The world-famous department store. Originally a grocer's shop in 1849 using a small section of the present-day site. It claims to provide 'anything within reason'. *Open 10.00-18.00 Mon, Tue & Sat, 10.00-19.00 Wed, Thur & Fri.*

HMS Belfast   5 F4

Morgans Lane, Tooley St SE1. 071-407 6434. Cruiser built for the Royal Navy; launched in 1938, it played an important role in the Battle of Northcape in December 1943. Now it's a permanent museum showing the role of this naval vessel in wartime. Little has changed since it was in active service. You can visit almost the whole ship including the engine room, boiler room, the bridge, mess decks and even the punishment cells. Film shows, lectures and quiz sheets for pre-booked groups. Not a recommended trip for the very young as there are lots of steps to climb. *Open Mar-Oct 10.00-18.00 Mon-Sun; Nov-Feb 10.00-17.00 Mon-Sun. Last ticket 45 minutes before closing.* Charge (special rates for parties of 10 or more).

Horse Guards Parade   4 F4

Whitehall SW1. Started in 1750 by William Kent, it took 10

years to complete. Used for ceremonies, tournaments and parades, as well as the daily Changing of the Guard *(11.00 Mon-Sat* and *10.00 Sun)*. Trooping the Colour to celebrate the Queen's official birthday also takes place here.

Houses of Parliament   **4 F5**

St Margaret St SW1. 071-219 3000. The kings and queens of England lived at the Palace of Westminster until the 1500s and from here they ruled the country with the help of advisors. These meetings became known as 'parliament', a word that means 'place for talking'. In 1834 most of the old Palace of Westminster was destroyed by fire. Westminster Hall is one of the few remaining parts of the original medieval palace. It has an impressive hammerbeam roof decorated with massive carved angels. A competition was held to design a new building and Charles Barry and A.W.N. Pugin were the winning architects, resulting in the Houses of Parliament we know today. It contains 1100 apartments, 100 staircases, 11 courtyards and over 2 miles of passages – quite some feat.

The old palace included the Royal Chapel of St Stephen, which ceased to be a chapel during the Reformation and became the meeting place of the House of Commons. The opposing parties face each other as though in the original choir stalls and the speaker sits where the altar would have been. No monarch has been allowed to enter the House of Commons since 1642 when Charles I burst in attempting to arrest five members but found that they had already flown.

The Lords first sat in the house in 1847. This house must still approve laws passed by the Commons, except financial, before they become statutory. The House of Lords is also the highest court in the land where final appeals are heard each week. The Lord Chancellor presides from his seat just below the throne of the woolsack; a reminder of the days when Britain's wealth depended on the wool trade. The famous Big Ben is the huge bell clock you can see in St Stephen's Tower. When Parliament is sitting at night, a light shines above the clock.

Admission to the House of Commons during debates is by application to your MP or by queueing at the St Stephen's entrance (there are always long queues in summer). Tours of Westminster Hall and the Palace of Westminster also by application to your MP. Free.

Kensington Palace   **3 C4**

Kensington Gardens W8. 071-937 9561. Bought by William III and altered by the architects Christopher Wren and William Kent. Queen Victoria was born at the palace and it was here, on 20 June 1837, that she was told she had become Queen. The state rooms were opened to the public in 1899 by Queen Victoria to commemorate her 80th birthday. The state apartments are full of 17th-century furniture and pictures and a costume museum with all the uniforms worn at court from the late 19th century onwards. Apartments are still used by members of the royal family. *Open Apr-Oct 09.00-17.30 Mon-Sat, 11.00-17.30 Sun; Nov-Mar 09.00-17.00 Mon-Sat, 11.00-17.00 Sun (last admission 16.15). Closed Bank hols and Xmas.* Charge.

Kenwood House (Iveagh Bequest)
Hampstead Lane NW3. 081-348 1286. Designed by Robert Adam in 1767-9. Full of 18th-century paintings and furniture. Look out for paintings by many of the old masters like Rembrandt, Hals and Vermeer. Gardens and wooded estate of 81 hectares (200 acres). Refreshments in the coach house. *Open Apr-Sep 10.00-18.00 Mon-Sun; Oct-Mar 10.00-16.00 Mon-Sun.* Free.

Kew Palace
Royal Botanical Gardens, Kew Rd, Richmond, Surrey. 081-781 9540. Small red-brick house in Dutch style, originally the country home of a London merchant and sometimes known as the Dutch House. In 1802 George III and Queen Charlotte used it while they awaited the building of a new summer palace. *Open Apr-Sep 11.00-17.30 Mon-Sun.* Gardens *open 09.30-dusk Mon-Sun.* Charge.

Lambeth Palace   7 F1
Lambeth Palace Rd SE1. 071-928 8282. The London residence of the Archbishop of Canterbury since 1197. Remarkable Tudor gatehouse and a medieval crypt. Also a 14th-century hall with portraits of past archbishops on its walls. The Great Hall, which houses the library, was rebuilt in medieval style in 1633. Even the gloves worn by Charles I when he went to the scaffold are on display.
Look out for the famous spreading fig tree, planted during Mary Tudor's reign by the last Catholic archbishop, Cardinal Pole; the brass plate commemorating the negligence of a gardener who put his fork through Archbishop Laud's tortoise and the picture of the original nosy Parker – archbishop under Elizabeth I and the first to have no allegiance to Rome – so called because he had a big nose. *Tours on Wed or Thur at 14.15 by written application to the Booking Secretary. Book well in advance – approx 18 months.*

Law Courts   5 A2
Strand WC2. 071-936 6000. Massive Victorian building, housing the Royal Courts of Justice. *Children must be over 14. Open to the public 09.00-16.30 Mon-Fri. Courts not in session Aug & Sep but still open to the public.* Free.

Lincoln's Inn 5 B2

Chancery Lane WC1. One of the Inns of Court dating back to 1422. The name comes from the Earl of Lincoln who had a town house here in the 1300s. The Old Buildings lead

---

London Bridges

The tidal Thames has 17 bridges; look out for the following:

Albert Bridge 6 E4

Unusual rigid chain suspension which makes it look like a giant iron cobweb. Beautifully lit up at night. Built by Ordish in 1875.

London Bridge 5 E4

The site of many replacements. It was a wooden construction until the 13th century. This was followed by the famous stone bridge which carried houses and shops and even the heads of executed traitors and criminals, displayed at the bridge gate. A granite bridge was built in 1832 but now lies in Lake Havasu City, Arizona, shipped off in 1971 and reassembled stone by stone. The latest construction was completed in 1973.

Tower Bridge 5 G4

Enter this fairy-tale bridge by the tower closest to the Tower of London and take a lift to the high walkways for superb views of London and the Thames when you visit 'The Celebration Story' – the Tower Bridge exhibition. See *Museums & Galleries* on page 49.

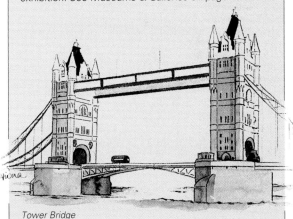

Tower Bridge

through to New Square where Dickens worked as a clerk when he was about 11. He also set the opening scene of *Bleak House* in the Old Hall of Lincoln's Inn.

London Wall   5 D1

Surviving parts of the Roman and medieval wall around the old city of London can still be seen at St Alphage on the north side of London Wall EC2; St Giles Churchyard, Cripplegate EC1; Jewry Street EC3; off Trinity Square EC3; and in the Tower of London EC3.

Mansion House   5 E2

Walbrook EC4. 071-626 2500. Opposite the Bank of England stands the official residence of the Lord Mayor. Has a rich and interesting Egyptian Hall which is worth visiting. *Open by application only. To arrange tours write in advance to the Principal Assistant's office (above address) stating preferred dates and times. Tours (min 15, max 40) by arrangement 11.00 & 14.00 Tue-Thur. Minimum age 12.* Free.

Marble Arch   4 A3

W1. Designed by John Nash in 1827, it was intended to be a grand new entrance for Buckingham Palace. It wasn't until it was finished that it was discovered that the arch was too narrow for the state coach to pass through so it had to be moved to its present site. From the 14th century to 1783 this was the spot for the Tyburn Gallows, the main execution site where hangings took place watched by excited crowds.

Merchant Taylor's Hall   5 E2

30 Threadneedle St EC2. 071-588 7606. This is the only Livery Hall which retains traces of its medieval origins. The City Livery Companies began as crafts guilds and were first recorded in England in 1180. They had monopoly powers in the Middle Ages, controlling prices, quality, wages, employees and working conditions. The guilds became known as Livery Companies due to the distinctive clothing, or 'livery', worn by their members. Twelve Companies, pre-eminent in medieval times, still exist and are known as 'Great Companies', the others are 'Minor'. A Master and one or two Wardens reside. Today, the Companies only rarely play a trading role, charitable and educational work being their chief functions. *Open by appointment for groups only by writing to the Clerk at the above address.* Free.

Nelson's Column   4 F4

Trafalgar Sq WC2. 44-metre (145ft) high granite column by William Railton, 1840, weighing 16 tonnes. On the top is a 5-metre (16ft) high statue of Nelson.

Old Bailey 5 C2

Old Bailey EC4. 071-248 3277. The Central Criminal Court, built on the site of the old Newgate Prison. Trials open to the public (see *Behind the Scenes* on page 61). Gallery *open 10.30-13.00 & 14.00-16.00 Mon-Fri. Minimum age 14 (must be accompanied by an adult until 16)*. Free.

Old Royal Observatory

Greenwich Park SE10. 081-858 4422. Formerly the Greenwich Observatory, this is Britain's oldest scientific institution, part of the National Maritime Museum. Designed by Wren and founded by Charles II in 1675. *Open Apr-Oct 10.00-18.00 Mon-Sat, 14.00-18.00 Sun; Nov-Mar 10.00-17.00 Mon-Sat, 14.00-17.00 Sun.* Charge.

Royal Albert Hall 3 E5

Kensington Gore SW7. 071-589 8212. It is oval, not circular as you might imagine. The design was based on Roman amphitheatres and was built to be a Hall of Arts and Sciences. The dome spans 56 metres by 67 metres (185ft by 219ft) and is 42.5 metres (135ft) high. Home of the Henry Wood Promenade Concerts (Proms) every year.

Royal Exchange 5 E2

Corner of Threadneedle St and Cornhill EC3. 071-623 0444. Built in 1884 by Tite. Originally founded as a market for merchants and craftsmen in 1564, and destroyed in the Great Fire. The second building was also burnt down in 1838.

Royal Naval College

Greenwich SE10. 081-858 2154. The site of the former royal palace of the Tudor kings and queens. It took Sir James Thornhill 20 years to paint the amazing hall in Sir Christopher Wren's building. During Cromwell's Commonwealth it was stripped of its furniture and turned into a biscuit factory! *Open 14.30-17.00 Mon-Sun. Closed Thur.* Free.

St James's Palace 4 D4

Pall Mall SW1. Built by Henry VIII for Anne Boleyn with many later additions. It is still officially a Royal residence and foreign ambassadors and High Commissioners are accredited to the Court of St James. It became the principal London residence of the sovereign after the destruction of Whitehall Palace. The original Tudor gatehouse is the main entrance to the palace. Notice the initials of Anne Boleyn and Henry VIII over the gatehouse door. The ceiling of the royal chapel was painted by Holbein, the famous court artist. *No admission to palace. Entry to courtyards only.* Free.

St Paul's Cathedral 5 D2

Ludgate Hill EC4. 071-248 2705. The old cathedral was completely destroyed in the Great Fire of London in 1666. The architect, Sir Christopher Wren, was commmissioned to rebuild St Paul's with its superb dome, porches and monuments. The dome is the second largest in the world after St Peter's in the Vatican; it is actually made of two domes, one inside the other. Running around the inside is a balcony called the Whispering Gallery. It gets its name because a whisper directed along the wall on one side of the dome can be heard very clearly on the other. The stalls are by Grinling Gibbons and the ironwork by Tijou. *To arrange tours telephone or write to Sightseeing Tours, Chapter House, St Paul's Churchyard EC4 071-236 0752, stating preferred dates and times. Tours at 11.00, 11.30, 13.30 & 14.00 Mon-Sat. Open 07.15-18.00 Mon-Sun (08.30-14.15* for sightseeing); *the Crypt is open 08.45-16.15 Mon-Sat;* the Galleries are *open 10.00-16.15 Mon-Sat.* Charge.

Southwark Cathedral   **5 E4**
Borough High St SE1. 071-407 2939. Built by Augustinian Canons in 1220, this is the earliest Gothic church in London. Beautiful choir stalls built in the Early English style. One of the earliest English poets, John Gower, who died in 1408, has a colourful tomb here. There is also a 20th-century memorial to Shakespeare. *Open 08.30-18.00 Mon-Sun (from 07.30 Tue).*

Thames Barrier Visitor Centre
Unity Way, Eastmoor St SE18. 081-854 1373. Examine the Thames Barrier, one of the most distinctive pieces of industrial architecture on the Thames, and find out how it works. There's an exhibition, a film show on the history of the river and why the barrier was built, and a video about its construction. For a close-up look take the *25-minute* Barrier cruise from Barrier Pier beside the visitor centre. *Open 10.00-17.00 Mon-Fri, 10.00-17.30 Sat, Sun & Bank hols. Closed Xmas and New Year.* Charge.

Tower of London   **5 G3**
Tower Hill EC3. 071-709 0765. This grim-looking fortress was begun by William the Conqueror in 1078. It has played a central role in some of the most dramatic episodes in English history. The White Tower, as it is now called, stood in isolation for 100 years and this is why the entire complex of 20 towers is still known as the Tower of London rather than the Castle of London, which it effectively is. The Tower has been most famous as a prison; many people such as Lady Jane Grey, Sir Walter Raleigh and Rudolf Hess have been locked away here to await their fate. Executions were carried out in the Tower and the list of famous people who

Tower of London

met their deaths in this way include Sir Thomas More, Anne Boleyn, whose head was chopped off with a sword, and the Countess of Salisbury, who had her head cut off while she was standing up. Along one wall, on the side nearest to the river, look for a building called the Bloody Tower. It takes its name from the murder of the two child princes here in 1483. Edward I's Medieval Palace has been restored, and costumed interpreters help recreate the atmosphere of Edward's court in the 1280s. Videos in the new Jewel House show the 1953 Coronation and detailed television pictures of the jewels. The crown jewels themselves can be seen at close range from two moving walkways. The collection includes St Edward's crown, used for the coronation ceremony, and the imperial state crown containing 3000 precious jewels. The gentlemen in Tudor uniform are the Yeomen Warders, a company founded by Henry VII in 1485. There are 39 of them and their task is to guard the Tower. They are sometimes known as 'Beefeaters'. There are also six ravens which guard the Tower and tradition has it that if the ravens leave, the Tower will fall. *Open Mar-Oct 09.00-18.00 Mon-Sat, 10.00-18.00 Sun; Nov-Feb 09.00-17.00 Mon-Sat, 10.00-17.00 Sun.* Charge.

Trafalgar Square   **4 E4**

WC2. The square honours Nelson, who went to sea at the age of 12 and was an Admiral by 39. He was killed in the Battle of Trafalgar in 1805. Nelson stands on his 44-metre

Trafalgar Square

(145ft) high column looking down Whitehall towards Old Admiralty. Famous for pigeons, political rallies and New Year's Eve revellers.

Westminster Abbey   **4 F6**

Broad Sanctuary SW1. 071-222 5152. One of the most important religious centres in the country. Many kings, queens and famous people are buried here and it has been the scene of every royal coronation since William the Conqueror in 1066. The original church was built by Edward the Confessor in 1065. During the 12th century the Abbey grew to its present splendour, partly because it established a cult of Edward the Confessor as a saint and attracted pilgrims to his tomb. The Henry VII Chapel was added in 1503 with its wonderful fan vaulting. The Abbey contains the coronation chair and many tombs and memorials of the kings and queens of England, British heroes, statesmen and poets. It is such an enormous place it is easiest to explore if you divide it into three: Edward the Confessor's Chapel, Henry VII's Chapel and the Abbey of the 'Commoners'. Underneath the Abbey is a small museum. It has plans, seals, charters, prints and documents together with wax funeral effigies of British monarchs including Elizabeth I, Mary Tudor and the 1.9-metre (6ft 2in) high figure of Charles II. *Open 09.00-16.00 Mon-Fri, 09.00-14.00 & 15.45-17.00 Sat. Closed Sun; services only.* Museum *open 10.30-16.00 Mon-Sun.* Free (charge for Royal Chapels and Museum).

★ *Houses of Famous People* ★ ★ ★ ★ ★

As you stroll around London, you'll see that some buildings have blue plaques on them. They are to show where famous people such as poets, artists, politicians, generals etc have lived or worked. There are over 400 round London. Below are listed houses that belonged to famous people and that are now open to the public.

Baden-Powell's House   **3 D5**
9 Hyde Park Gate SW7. Robert Baden-Powell, founder of the Boy Scouts, lived here from 1861-76. On the corner of Queen's Gate and Cromwell Road (**6 C2**) is the Baden-Powell Museum where a small exhibition illustrates the history of the founding of the movement with photographs and relics. 071-584 7030. Museum *open 07.00-23.00 Mon-Sun*. Free.

Dickens' House   **2 B5**
48 Doughty St WC1. 071-405 2127. Dickens lived here from 1837-9 during which time he completed *The Pickwick Papers* and wrote *Oliver Twist* and *Nicholas Nickleby*. Among the fascinating exhibits on display is the Dickens family tree, his desk, chair and china monkey, without which he couldn't start work. *Open 10.00-17.00 Mon-Sat (last admission 16.30). Closed Sun & Bank hols*. Charge.

Freud Museum
20 Maresfield Gdns NW3. 071-435 2002. This was Freud's last home from 1938-9. He arrived here a refugee from the Nazis, bringing most of his possessions with him. The museum contains a major collection of the psychologist's personal effects: library, letters, antiquities and furniture including the famous couch on which psychoanalysis was pioneered. *Open 12.00-17.00 Wed-Sun*. Charge.

Hogarth's House
Hogarth Lane, Great West Rd W4. 081-994 6757. The 17th-century country villa (if you can believe it with the Great West Road thundering past!) of William Hogarth, the well-known painter and illustrator. The house is full of all his personal mementoes, relics and impressions of his engravings. *To arrange tours individuals and small groups do not need to book; just call at the house during opening hours. Large groups should telephone or write in advance. Open Apr-Sep 11.00-18.00 Mon & Wed-Sat, 14.00-18.00 Sun; Oct-Mar 11.00-16.00 Mon & Wed-Sat, 14.00-16.00 Sun. Closed Tue, first two weeks of Sep & last three weeks of Dec*. Free.

Dr Johnson's House   **5 B2**
17 Gough Sq, Fleet St EC4. 071-353 3745. Johnson, who compiled the first English dictionary, lived in this 17th-

century house from 1748-59. *Open May-Sep 11.00-17.30 Mon-Sat; Oct-Apr 11.00-17.00 Mon-Sat. Closed Sun & Bank hols.* Charge.

Keats' House

Wentworth Pl, Keats Grove NW3. 071-435 2062. The poet, John Keats, lived here from 1818-20. It was here that Keats produced his greatest poetry including *Ode to a Nightingale, La Belle Dame sans Merci* and *Ode to a Grecian Urn. To arrange tours, individuals phone in advance to join a group tour; groups phone in advance to obtain a booking form (above address). Open May-Oct 10.00-13.00 & 14.00-18.00 Mon-Fri, 10.00-13.00 & 14.00-17.00 Sat, 14.00-17.00 Sun; Nov-Apr 13.00-17.00 Mon-Fri, 10.00-13.00 & 14.00-17.00 Sat, 14.00-17.00 Sun.* Charge.

William Morris Gallery

Lloyd Park, Forest Rd E17. 081-527 3782. Eighteenth-century house of the designer, poet and craftsman. Textiles, wallpapers, carpets, woodwork and designs by Morris and his pre-Raphaelite contemporaries are housed in Morris' boyhood home. *Open 10.00-13.00 & 14.00-17.00 Tue-Sat, 10.00-12.00 & 14.00-17.00 first Sun in the month. Closed Mon & Bank hols.* Free.

Wellington Museum   **4 B5**

Apsley House, 149 Piccadilly W1. 071-499 5676. Originally known as 'Number One London', the home of one of Britain's most famous generals, the Duke of Wellington. Built 1771-8 from designs by Robert Adam and altered in 1828 by B.D. Wyatt. Contains Wellington's relics, fine Spanish and Dutch paintings (including Goya's *Wellington on Horseback* and Caravaggio's *Agony in the Garden),* silver plate and porcelain. Charge. *Closed for refurbishment at time of publication.*

★ Museums & Galleries

London is one of the richest cities in the world when it comes to museums and galleries, and many of the capital's museums have special features of particular interest to children. Some have educational events or programmes, such as quizzes, trails, lectures and film shows, or project sheets which have information and activities based on the displays. For more detailed information contact the individual museum's Educational Officer.

Some of the following are well known and you will undoubtedly have heard of them, but we have also listed some which are not so famous and which are full of surprising treasures and oddities. The following categories are designed to help you find exactly what you are looking for:

★ *Science and Nature* ★ ★ ★ ★ ★ ★ ★ ★

Natural History Museum   6 D1
(& Geological Museum)
Cromwell Road SW7. 071-938 9123. The Natural History Museum was designed by Alfred Waterhouse and incorporates the Geological Museum. The Natural History Museum houses a huge collection of animal and plant specimens; if you don't know where to start, follow one of the nature trails. On the way round you can take a close look at our feathered friends, cases of bright butterflies and evil-looking spiders. The central hall houses dinosaurs, including the massive skeleton of one of the largest land animals, the dinosaur Diplodocus. Just as spectacular is the full-scale model of the biggest animal alive today – the blue whale. It is longer than three double-decker buses. There are all sorts of push-button machines to help you understand how your body works, for example how the nervous system functions. There is also a family centre where you can do anything from touching a python's skin to examining a butterfly's wings under a microscope. Activity sheets available.
The Geological Museum houses a massive collection of gold, diamonds, minerals, rocks and fossils as well as an

impressive collection of gem stones. Don't miss the earthquake simulator, a moving platform which gives you the same feeling as being in a real earth tremor. Special activities in *school holidays and half-terms*. Lectures and demonstrations can be organised for school parties – *phone the Education Department in advance for details*. Both Natural History and Geological Museums *open 10.00-18.00 Mon-Sat, 11.00-18.00 Sun*. Charge (*16.30-18.00 Mon-Fri, 17.00-18.00 Sat & Sun* free).

Science Museum   **6 D1**
Exhibition Rd SW7. 071-938 8000. Exhibitions to help you unravel the mysteries of science. Highlights of the collection include a 1797 Watts beam engine, the real Apollo 10 launch module and the oldest locomotive in the world. In the basement the children's gallery has working models demonstrating scientific principles. At the Launch Pad you can build a bridge, be a human battery or try out many other challenging experiments. The Sainsbury Gallery explains the impact of science on today's food with hands-on displays like the Food Pyramid and computer-driven exhibits. The Wellcome Museum of the History of Medicine reconstructs important events in medical history and has a wealth of fascinating objects. The Flight gallery records the history of aeronautics from impossible Renaissance dreams to the air transport system of today. *Open 10.00-18.00 Mon-Sat, 11.00-18.00 Sun*. Charge.

Story of Telecommunications   **5 D3**
145 Queen Victoria St EC4. 071-248 7444. British Telecom museum chronicles the rise of telecommunications from the invention of the telegraph, through the development of the telephone, to the age of digital transmission and the fax. Modern displays full of flashing lights and the sound of clicking switchgear, ringing phones and video soundtracks. *Open 10.00-17.00 Mon-Fri*. Free.

★ *Fun and Fear* ★ ★ ★ ★ ★ ★ ★ ★ ★ ★ ★

Guinness World of Records   **4 E3**
Trocadero Centre, Piccadilly Circus W1. 071-439 7331. Brings to life dozens of amazing facts from the Guinness Book of Records. You'll find things like life-sized models of the tallest and heaviest men and a recreation of Noah's Ark with record-breaking information. Find out which is the sleepiest, the smelliest or the warmest creature in the animal kingdom. Special visits can be arranged for schools

with worksheets provided. *Open 10.00-22.00 Mon-Sun.*
Charge (under 5s free).

House of Detention   **2 C5**
Clerkenwell Close EC1. 071-253 9494. The story of three
centuries of crime and punishment in London and
Clerkenwell. Includes a guided tour of the maze of eerie tun-
nels, cells and passageways of the underground prison.
Open 10.00-18.00 Mon-Sun.

London Dungeon   5 E4
34 Tooley St SE1. 071-403 0606. A medieval horror museum with a gruesomely realistic exhibition of sacrifices, tortures, plagues, murders and executions in the vaults under London Bridge Station. *Not suitable for young children. For advance group bookings phone 071-403 7221. Open 10.00-16.30 Mon-Sun.* Charge.

Madame Tussaud's   1 C5
Marylebone Rd NW1. 071-935 6861. Amongst the waxwork effigies of the famous and notorious meet the Royal Family, Pavarotti, Nelson Mandela and Cher. The figures are life-sized and dressed with great attention to detail, right down to their buttons. Murderers lurk in the Chamber of Horrors, which is genuinely gruesome with figures of evil-looking villains and a real guillotine and gallows (unsuitable for young children). Mingle with celebrities at 'The Garden Party'. Enjoy the sights and sounds of the seaside at 'The Promenade Pier Café'. Experience some of the greatest events that have shaped London's heritage at 'The Spirit of London', Madame Tussaud's newest exhibition where visitors journey through 400 years of London's history in a replica of a black taxi cab. Very busy in *Jul* and *Aug. Open 10.00-17.30 Mon-Fri, 09.30-17.30 Sat & Sun.* Charge (combined ticket with Planetarium available).

Planetarium   1 C5
Marylebone Rd NW1. 071-486 1121. Boggle your mind with stories of stars, space and the cosmos. It's just like being outdoors on a clear night only you've got an expert guide to explain the mysteries of it all. Tickets include entry into the 'Space Trail', the new lift-off zone where you go on an exciting voyage of discovery into space before taking your seats for the star show. Shows *every 40 minutes Mon-Sun.* First show *10.20;* last show *17.00.* Charge (combined ticket with Madame Tussaud's available). No children under 5.

Rock Circus   4 E3
London Pavilion, Piccadilly W1. 071-734 8025. The skills and artistry of Madame Tussaud's combine with audio animatronic techniques to bring the great rock stars to life in a unique performance. Features robots, waxworks, lasers, lighting and superb personal stereo sound. See Elvis, The Beatles and Madonna. *Open 11.00-21.00 Mon, Wed, Thur & Sun, 12.00-21.00 Tue, 12.00-22.00 Fri & Sat.* Charge.

Sherlock Holmes Museum   1 B5
221b Baker St NW1. 071-935 8866. Said to be the actual house on which Conan Doyle modelled his imaginary 221b. The great detective's domestic world has been recreated

based on detailed study of the stories. See Holmes' cluttered sitting room and bedroom, full of personal touches. In Dr Watson's room you can sit by the fire and read the stories and period magazines. *Open 09.30-18.00 Mon-Sun.* Charge.

★ *People and History* ★ ★ ★ ★ ★ ★ ★ ★ ★

British Museum   4 F1
Great Russell St WC1. 071-636 1555. (Recorded information: 071-580 1788.) Pick up a copy of British Museum Information and Plans to help you find your way around the wealth of treasures here. But it doesn't really matter in the least if you get lost as every room has something of interest. Founded in 1753, the British Museum is one of the great museums of the world, showing the works of man from prehistoric times to the present day. The museum houses ancient objects from many historic civilisations, including Ancient Egypt, Greece and Roman Britain as well as smaller collections from China and India. The exhibits are so rich and varied that you should not attempt to see them all in a single visit.

The museum is famous for its Egyptian mummies – in rooms 60 & 61 you can see mummies of Kings, Queens and their servants.The Duveen Gallery (room 8) holds the Elgin Marbles from the Parthenon in Athens. They show the birth of Athena and procession to honour her. The Sutton Hoo treasure in room 41 comes from the burial site of a 7th-century anglo-saxon king in Suffolk. He was buried in a ship along with a rich treasure hoard to use in the after-life.

The British Library forms part of the museum. It has over 110 miles of shelves and over 10 million books in store. In *school hols* there are special talks and activities for 8-13 year-olds. *Phone for details. Open 10.00-17.00 Mon-Sat, 14.30-18.00 Sun.* Films, lectures *Tue-Sat*, gallery talks. Free (charge for special exhibitions and guided tours).

Commonwealth Institute   3 B6
230 Kensington High St W8. 071-603 4535. A modern building like a great glass tent. Discover the history, landscapes, wildlife and crafts of the Commonwealth on three floors of magical galleries which have continuous and changing exhibitions on every Commonwealth country, associated state and dependency. There are also cultural events and exhibitions, and special educational programmes. *Phone for details.* Shop and coffee house. *Open 10.00-17.00 Mon-Sat, 14.00-17.00 Sun. Closed Bank hols.* Charge.

Geffrye Museum   2 G3

Kingsland Rd E2. 071-739 9893. A folk museum with a difference. This small museum has a series of rooms which have been decorated in period styles from the 1600s to the 1950s, showing how homes looked in the past. For example, there's an 18th-century woodworker's shop and an open hearth kitchen. Each of the rooms is typical of the way we once lived. The museum and gardens are brought to life through drama, music, workshops and seminars. *Open 10.00-17.00 Tue-Sat, 14.00-17.00 Sun. Closed Mon except Bank hols.* Walled Herb Garden *open Apr-Oct.*

Horniman Museum

100 London Road, Forest Hill SE23. 081-699 2339. Tucked away in south London, the Horniman Museum houses a huge collection of unusual objects, including Egyptian mummies and masks, a stuffed walrus and a vivarium with snakes and lizards. In the new Music Room, instruments of all periods come alive at the touch of a computer key. The collections here grew out of Frederick J Horniman's hoarding instincts. He was a tea magnate who travelled the world collecting bits and pieces. Children's workshop provides crafts and drawing materials. There are three nature trails in the surrounding garden. Special exhibitions. Museum *open 10.30-17.30 Mon-Sat, 14.00-17.30 Sun.* Free. Children's workshops *during school hols and on Sat during term time. Limited numbers – phone for details.*

Museum of London   5 D1

London Wall EC2. 071-600 3699. Tells the story of London from the earliest times. Rooms are arranged chronologically and every item, from Roman silverwork to a 1920s Art Deco lift from Selfridges, reveals something about our ancestors' industry. See the devastation of the Great Fire and look at models of Victorian shops. School holiday projects organised. *Open 10.00-18.00 Tue-Sat, 12.00-18.00 Sun. Closed Mon.* Charge.

Museum of Mankind   4 D3

6 Burlington Gdns W1. 071-437 2224. A series of changing exhibitions on the life and culture of non-Western societies to portray the entire way of life of a particular people. Collections come from the indigenous peoples of Africa, Australia, the Pacific islands, North and South America and parts of Asia and Europe. You can take a close look at the lifestyles, costumes, homes and crafts. There are free filmshows on *Tue-Fri afternoons*, linked to the current exhibitions. Worksheets available. *Open 10.00-17.00 Mon-Sat, 14.30-18.00 Sun. Closed some Bank hols.* Free.

Ragged School Museum

46-48 Copperfield Rd E3. 081-980 6405. Photographs, documents and objects concerned with the lives of the children who attended Dr Barnardo's Free Ragged Schools which he started in the 1877. Attend a Victorian school lesson in the recreated classroom. Changing programme of exhibitions. *Open 10.00-17.00 Wed & Thur and 14.00-17.00 first Sun of the month.* Free (voluntary donation).

Tower Hill Pageant   5 G3

1 Tower Hill Terrace EC3. 071-709 0081. London's first 'darkride' museum where an automated car takes you on a journey through converted wine vaults near the Tower of London. The Pageant focuses on the riverside port area and depicts scenes from 2000 years of London's history. See Londoners fleeing in panic before the Great Fire of 1666 and get a bird's eye view of the city from a German bomber as it blitzed the docks in 1940. *Open Apr-Oct 09.30-17.30 Mon-Sun; Nov-Mar 09.30-16.30 Mon-Sun.* Charge.

★ *London at Work* ★ ★ ★ ★ ★ ★ ★ ★ ★ ★

Bank of England Museum   5 E2

Bank of England, Bartholomew Lane EC2. 071-601 5545. Charts the Bank's history from the Royal Charter, granted in 1694, to the high-tech world of modern banking. There are collections of Roman gold bars,unique banknotes and an opportunity to look behind the doors of the Bank with an interactive video. You can also experience the excitement of the Dealing Desk as it gives live information on gilt-edged stocks and securities. Films, question and answer sessions, lectures. Special activities for children and presentations for booked groups. *Open 10.00-17.00 Mon-Fri, 11.00-17.00 Sat & Sun; Oct-Easter closed Sat.* Free.

Kew Bridge Steam Museum

Green Dragon Lane, Brentford, Middx. 081-568 4757. A pumping station with six large steam-driven water pumping engines in working order. They were used for a long time to pump water from the Thames into London's reservoir system. Lifts 2800 litres (280 gallons) of water at one seemingly effortless stroke. Steamed up each weekend for the benefit of visitors. Also a working forge, a steam railway and models. The museum is *open 11.00-17.00 Mon-Sun.* Charge (under 5s free).

London Fire Brigade Museum   **5 D5**
94a Southwark Bridge Rd SE1. 071-587 2894. Exhibits fire-fighting gear from the 17th-century to the present. You can see the old uniforms and leather buckets that were once used. By appointment only and not recommended for children under ten years of age. *Open 09.30-16.00 Mon-Fri*. Charge.

London Transport Museum   **4 G3**
The Piazza, Covent Garden WC2. 071-379 6344. Recently refurbished, the museum tells the story of London's public transport system and its effect on life in the capital since 1800. Exciting displays of buses, trams, trains and posters with 'hands-on' touch screen displays, videos and working models. Actors, exhibitions and guided tours. Café, shop and information centre. *Open 10.00-18.00 (last admission 17.15) Mon-Sun*. Charge.

National Postal Museum   **5 D2**
King Edward Building, King Edward St EC1. 071-239 5420. Superb display of stamps. Houses the Philips collection and the 'Berne' collection of almost every stamp or piece of postal stationery issued anywhere in the world since 1878 including the famous Penny Black. However good your own collection, you'll be green with envy at the sight of this one. Reference library. *Open 09.30-16.30 Mon-Fri. Closed Bank hols*. Free.

Royal Mews   **4 C6**
Buckingham Palace Rd SW1. 071-930 4832. The Queen's horses are on view here plus the royal and state carriages including the gold coach and the glass coach. The gold state coach has been used for every coronation since George IV. It is 8 metres (24ft) long and weighs 4 tonnes and when in use is drawn by 8 horses. The glass coach is used for royal weddings. *Open Jan-Mar 12.00-16.00 Wed; Apr-Sep 12.00-16.00 Tue-Thur; Oct-Dec 12.00-16.00 Wed; except on state occasions. Last admission 15.30*. Charge.

Tower Bridge Museum   **5 G4**
Tower Bridge SE1. 071-407 0922. The most fairy-tale bridge to span the Thames with excellent views from its high walkways. 'The Celebration Story' brings to life the history, human endeavour and engineering achievement which created this famous landmark. Find out why the bridge was built and how the design was arrived at; how the bridge generated its own hydraulic power; what it was like in the steam engine room. Compare today's skyline with that of 1894 and join in the celebrations of the Royal Opening

Tower Bridge

which took place on 30 June 1894 via a light, sound and vision show. *Open Apr-Oct 10.00-18.30 Mon-Sun; Nov-Mar 10.00-17.15 Mon-Sun.* Charge.

★ *Toys and Models* ★ ★ ★ ★ ★ ★ ★ ★ ★ ★ ★

Bethnal Green Museum of Childhood
Cambridge Heath Rd E2. 081-980 2415. An enchanting collection of dolls' houses, dolls, toys, puppets and children's costumes originally housed in the Victoria and Albert Museum. It's nearly as good as a toy shop. In the museum shop you can buy replicas of old-fashioned games and toys. A regular *Saturday* workshop for children provides facilities for drawing, puppetry, story-telling and Punch & Judy shows with traditional figures. *Open 10.00-17.50 Mon-Thur & Sat,14.30-17.50 Sun. Closed Fri.* Free.

Cabaret Mechanical Theatre   **4 F3**
33-34 The Market, Covent Garden WC2. 071-379 7961. A unique collection of contemporary automata and mechanical sculpture in the former vegetable vaults of Covent Garden Market. Over 100 hand-carved, hand-painted moving models operated by push-button. Great fun for inquisitive children as the mechanics of the pieces are all exposed. *Open 10.00-18.30 Mon-Sun.* Charge.

London Toy & Model Museum   **3 D3**
21-23 Craven Hill W2. 071-262 9450. Crammed with all sorts of goodies from Victorian and Edwardian nurseries; a

tin toy collection, an historic selection of toys and models and a cross-section of a furnished Victorian dolls' house. In the garden are miniature working railways, including a ride-on train, a boating pond and a 56-seater bus. *Open 10.00-17.30 Tue-Sat, 11.00-17.30 Sun. Last admission 16.30.* Charge.

Pollock's Toy Museum 4 D1
1 Scala St W1. 071-636 3452. Three rickety floors of small, creaking rooms are packed with a magical mix of bygone toys – dolls, dolls' houses, teddies (be on the lookout for the oldest teddy in the world), tin toys, games, comics, puppets and modern space toys. Scale models and Pollock's own famous toy theatres are on sale on the ground floor. *Open 10.00-17.00 Mon-Sat (last admission 16.30). Closed Sun & some Bank hols.* Charge.

★ *Crafts and Design* ★ ★ ★ ★ ★ ★ ★ ★ ★

Crafts Council Gallery 2 C3
44a Pentonville Road N1. 071-278 7700. Changing exhibitions of contemporary crafts; also an information service on where to learn about or buy crafts; colour slide library which surveys the best of crafts in Britain. *Open 11.00-18.00 Tue-Sat, 14.00-18.00 Sun. Closed Mon & Bank hols.* Free (charge for special exhibitions).

Design Council 4 E3
28 Haymarket SW1. 071-839 8000. This is the public face of the government-sponsored Design Council, which promotes

the use of good design in British industry. Here you can see everything from cutlery and furniture to construction fittings for buildings. Upstairs is the Young Designers Centre, where design work by young people in all disciplines is displayed. *Open 10.00-18.00 Mon-Sat, 13.00-18.00 Sun.* Free.

Design Museum   5 G4
Butler's Wharf, Shad Thames SE1. 071-407 6261. Sponsored by the Conran Foundation, this museum's range of exhibits includes furniture, gadgets and graphics from cars to teapots. It aims to make everyone aware of design, past, present and future. Bookshop, café, restaurant, library and lecture theatre. *Open 10.30-17.30 Mon-Sun. Closed Mon.* Charge (free for schools booking in advance).

★ *Art Galleries* ★ ★ ★ ★ ★ ★ ★ ★ ★ ★ ★

Courtauld Institute Galleries   4 G3
Somerset House, Strand WC2. 071-873 2526. Home to the Courtauld Collection of French Impressionists and Post-Impressionists (including fine paintings by Cézanne, Van Gogh, Gauguin, Monet and Manet) and the Lee, Gambier-Parry and Fry Collections. The Princes Gate collection of Flemish and Italian Old Masters is on permanent exhibition. Not as crowded as some of the national galleries. *To arrange tours phone 071-873 2549 (Mon-Sat) in advance stating preferred dates. Open 10.00-18.00 Mon-Sat, 14.00-18.00 Sun.* Charge.

Dulwich Picture Gallery
College Rd SE21. 081-693 5254. English, Italian, Spanish, Dutch and French paintings exhibited in the oldest and one of the most beautiful art galleries in England. Keep an eye out for paintings by Rembrandt, Rubens, Murillo and Gainsborough. Building 1811-14 by Sir John Soane. *Tours at 15.00 Sat & Sun. Groups should telephone or write in advance (above address) stating preferred dates. Open 10.00-17.00 Tue-Fri, 10.00-17.00 Sat, 14.00-17.00 Sun. Closed Mon & Bank hols.* Small charge. Under 16s free.

Hayward Gallery   5 A4
South Bank SE1. 071-928 3144. (Recorded information: 071-261 0127.) This gallery can be picked out from the rest of the South Bank complex by the flashing neon light sculpture it wears on its head. Changing exhibitions of American, European and British art. *Open 10.00-18.00 Mon-Sun (to 20.00 Tue & Wed). Check in advance as closed in between exhibitions.* Charge.

Institute of Contemporary Arts (ICA)   4 E4
The Mall SW1. 071-930 3647. Three galleries in which changing exhibitions explore new ideas in contemporary art – can include anything from sculpture to photographs. Also two cinemas, theatre, bar, restaurant and bookshop. *Open 12.00-01.00 Mon-Sat, 12.00-22.30 Sun* (galleries *to 19.30)*. Small charge.

National Gallery   4 E3
Trafalgar Square WC2. 071-839 3321. Large collection including some world-famous paintings. Rich in early Italian paintings (Leonardo da Vinci, Raphael, Botticelli and Titian), Dutch and Flemish (Rembrandt, Rubens, Frans Hal and Van Dyck), Spanish (Velázquez and El Greco), British 18th and 19th century (Constable, Turner, Gainsborough and Reynolds). The Impressionist collection includes paintings by Van Gogh, Monet and Cézanne. An information sheet, *A Quick Visit to the National Gallery*, leads you to the 16 masterpieces. If dazed by all the possibilities join the daily guided tours which highlight selected pictures. The Education Department runs holiday quizzes and slide/tape shows to introduce you to this vast collection of paintings. *Open 10.00-18.00 Mon-Sat, 14.00-18.00 Sun.* Free.

National Portrait Gallery   4 F3
2 St Martin's Place WC2. 071-306 0055. Portraits of the famous and not so famous people throughout the ages. Find out what your favourite character in history looked like. There are over 9000 portraits in the primary collection from Henry VIII to Shakespeare (who looks strangely modern with an earring in his left ear) and Lawrence of Arabia to Mick Jagger. The collection also includes paintings, miniatures, sculptures, drawings, caricatures and photographs. Photography gallery. Special exhibitions are held regularly throughout the year. The Education Department runs children's holiday events like painting and study groups, usually in *Easter and summer hols*. Quiz and worksheets available. *Open 10.00-18.00 Mon-Sat, 12.00-18.00 Sun. Closed some Bank hols.* Free (charge for some special exhibitions).

Photographer's Gallery   4 E3
5 & 8 Great Newport St WC2. 071-831 1772. Exciting photographic exhibitions. Print room, coffee bar and bookshop. *Open 11.00-19.00 Tue-Sat. Closed Sun & Mon.* Free.

Queen's Gallery   4 C5
Buckingham Palace, Buckingham Palace Rd SW1. 071-930 4832. Pictures and works of art from all parts of the Royal Collection. Exhibitions change at intervals. *Open Mar-Dec 10.00-17.00 Tue-Sat, 14.00-17.00 Sun. Last admission*

16.30. Closed Mon except Bank hols and when the State Apartments are open. Charge.

Royal Academy of Arts   **4 D3**

Burlington House, Piccadilly W1. 071-439 7438. Holds major special loan exhibitions throughout the year. Probably most famous for its inspirational annual Summer Exhibition *May-Aug*, in which the works of living artists are displayed and in most cases are on sale. *Open 10.00-18.00 Mon-Sun. Last admission 17.30.* Charge.

Tate Gallery   **7 E2**

Millbank SW1. 071-887 8000. Sir Henry Tate, the inventor of sugar cubes, donated his own collection, together with £80,000 for a new building in 1891. Exhibits from 16th-century British art to contemporary world art. In the adjoining Clore Gallery hangs the Turner collection. The gallery shop is good for posters and postcards. Coffee shop. Trails and special children's tours *during term time and school hols – contact the Education Department for details. Open 10.00-17.50 Mon-Sat, 14.00-17.50 Sun.* Free (charge for special exhibitions).

Victoria & Albert Museum   **6 D1**

Cromwell Rd SW7. 071-938 8500. The V&A is Britain's National Museum of Art and Design and has one of the world's finest collections of furniture, ceramics and glass, metalwork and jewellery, textiles and dress from the Middle Ages to the 20th century, as well as paintings, prints, drawings, posters, photographs and sculpture. The Twentieth Century Gallery spans the history of consumer design from Mackintosh fireplaces and paper dresses to Swatch watches and Dr Marten shoes. There are also superb collections from China, Japan, India and the Middle East. If you don't know where to begin, various guidebooks are available from the museum shop. *Open 12.00-17.50 Mon, 10.00-17.50 Tue-Sun.* Free (donation requested).

★ *Theatre, Film and Music* ★ ★ ★ ★ ★

Museum of Instruments   **3 E6**

Royal College of Music, Prince Consort Rd SW7. O71-589 3643. Over 600 exhibits, mostly European keyboard, stringed and wind instruments from the 16th-19th centuries. A small section includes instruments from Japan, China, India, the Middle East and Africa. *Open 14.00-16.30 Wed (during term time) or by appointment with the Curator.* Charge.

Museum of the Moving Image (MOMI)   **5 B4**

Under Waterloo Bridge, South Bank SE1. 071-928 3535. Part of the South Bank complex, this exciting museum tells the history of moving images from Chinese shadow puppets to the beginnings of photography through to film, television, video, satellite and hologram technology. During the journey you can take part in lots of film and television-making processes to learn the technical and creative wizardry of the media. In the Moving Image workshop is a continuous programme of events; lectures, films and magic lantern shows. Study rooms available for groups. *Open 10.00-18.00 Mon-Sun. Last admission 17.00.* Charge.

Musical Museum
368 High St, Brentford, Middx. 081-560 8108. A fine collection of automatic musical instruments, including pianos, musical boxes and organs. Some of the pianos reproduce the playing of turn-of-the-century composers and musicians using special paper rolls and pneumatic systems. Also featured is a Wurlitzer theatre organ. *1½-hour* demonstration tour. *Open Apr-Jun 14.00-17.00 Sat & Sun only; Jul & Aug 14.00-16.00 Wed-Fri, 14.00-17.00 Sat & Sun; Sep-Oct 14.00-17.00 Sat & Sun only; closed Nov-Mar.* Charge.

Shakespeare Globe Museum   **5 D4**
1 Bear Gdns, Bankside SE1. 071-928 6342. Elizabethan theatre history, including a reconstruction of Shakespeare's first Globe theatre. Special events and activities. *Open 10.00-17.00 Mon-Sat, 14.00-17.30 Sun.* Charge.

Theatre Museum   **4 F3**
Russell St WC2. 071-836 7891. Covent Garden's old Flower Market has now been transformed into the Theatre Museum, an outpost of the V&A. It covers major developments, events and personalities from all the performing arts. It also houses curios such as the magic piano from *Salad Days* and Eliza Doolittle's gown from *My Fair Lady*. *Open 11.00-19.00 Tue-Sun. Closed Mon.* Charge.

★ *Service to the Nation* ★ ★ ★ ★ ★ ★ ★

Artillery Museum
The Rotunda, Repository Rd, Greenhill, Woowich SE18. 081-854 2242 ex 3128. The Rotunda was an architectural 'tent' originally erected in St James's Park in 1814 and later moved here. An amazing collection of guns and muskets, rifles, armour and even early rockets. *Open summer 12.00-17.00 Mon-Fri, 13.00-17.00 Sat & Sun; winter 12.00-16.00 Mon-Fri, 13.00-16.00 Sat & Sun.*

Cabinet War Rooms   **4 F5**
Clive Steps, King Charles St SW1. 071-930 6961.

Fascinating reconstruction of the underground emergency accommodation used by Winston Churchill, his War Cabinet and the Chiefs of Staff of Britain's armed forces during World War II. It was here that the progress of the war was plotted and monitored. You can see the desk from which the Prime Minister made some of his famous broadcasts and in a small room there's the original hot-line, the first telephone line with a scrambler used by Churchill to communicate with President Roosevelt. *To arrange tours phone or write well in advance to The Deputy Curator (above address); dates and times are at his discretion. Open 10.00-17.15 Mon-Sun.* Charge.

Florence Nightingale Museum   **7 F1**
2 Lambeth Palace Rd SE1. 071-620 0374. Museum within St Thomas's Hospital where 'the lady with the lamp' founded the first-ever school of nursing over 100 years ago. Contains many of her personal possessions including one of her famous lamps. Reconstruction of a ward in the Crimea. Audio-visual presentation of the history of nursing, midwifery and hospital work plus a series of changing exhibitions and events. *Open 10.00-16.00 Tue-Sun.* Charge.

Guards Museum   **4 D5**
Wellington Barracks, Birdcage Walk SW1. 071-414 3271. Tells the story of the five infantry regiments that make up the Guards Division – Coldstream, Grenadier, Scots, Irish and Welsh Guards. Exhibits of historic uniforms and bearskins, weapons, soldiers' personal possessions, war trophies, and other regimental curiosities. *Open 10.00-16.00 Mon-Sun (closed Fri).* Charge.

Imperial War Museum   **5 B6**
Lambeth Rd SE1. 071-416 5000. (Recorded information: 071-820 1683.) Very popular national museum illustrating every possible aspect of the two world wars with a vast collection of models, weapons, paintings and relics including a Mark I Spitfire and Heinkel from the Second World War. There's also the 'Blitz Experience' where you can see, feel and hear what it was like to be in London during the Blitz; 'Operation Jericho' where you can experience what it was like to fly with the RAF to release captured Resistance fighters, and the lifesize 'French Experience' where you can see the men 'going over the top'. Film shows *Sat & Sun.* Special exhibits and workshops for children *during school hols. Open 10.00-17.50 Mon-Sun.* Charge (free *after 16.30 daily*).

National Army Museum   **6 F3**
Royal Hospital Rd SW3. 071-730 0717. The story of the

British Army from 1485; its professional and social life all over the world. Uniforms, pictures, weapons and personal relics. See a 400sq ft model of the Battle of Waterloo with over 70,000 model soldiers; also a skeleton of Napoleon's horse. *Summer holiday* events include model making, drawing, trails, films and talks. Information available each *Jul* from the Education Department. *Open 10.00-17.30 Mon-Sun.* Free.

National Maritime Museum
Romney Rd SE10. 081-858 4422. The finest maritime collection of paintings, navigational instruments, costumes and weapons. Find out all about England's great sea-faring tradition. See Nelson's uniform from the Battle of Trafalgar. Next door is the Old Royal Observatory where most of the pioneer work in the development of astronomy and nautical navigation was done. Stand astride the Meridian Line. Reach for the sky in a dome which houses the largest refracting telescope in the UK. *Open Apr-Oct 10.00-18.00 Mon-Sat, 12.00-18.00 Sun; Nov-Mar 10.00-17.00 Mon-Sat, 14.00-17.00 Sun. Closed some Bank hols.* Charge.

Royal Air Force Museum
Grahame Park Way NW9. 081-205 2266. The first national museum covering all aspects of the RAF and its predecessor, the RFC. Plane spotters will particularly enjoy this impressive collection. It is on the site of an old airfield and all the exhibits are in former hangars. Aeroplanes, equipment, paintings and documents on show. There's also a flight simulator which will allow you to experience the thrill of flying in an RAF Tornado. The Battle of Britain Hall has British, German and Italian aircraft including a Spitfire, Hurricane and Messerschmitt and a *20-minute* video giving its complete story. The Bomber Command Hall is also incorporated into the RAF Museum. Cinema and shop. *Open 10.00-18.00 Mon-Sun.* Charge.

Winston Churchill's Britain at War Experience   5 F4
64-66 Tooley St SE1. 071-403 3171. Step back in time to the dark days of World War II for an unforgettable adventure that's fun and educational. Step into London underground where thousands slept and pick your way through the rubble of the London Blitz. Anderson shelter, gas masks, ration books and clothing coupons. *Open Apr-Sep 10.00-17.30 Mon-Sun; Oct-Mar 10.00-16.30 Mon-Sun.* Charge.

★ *Behind the Scenes*

A chance to see for yourself how things work. Some places offer organised tours or group visits – a good idea if you've got lots of questions to ask.

★ *Airports* ★ ★ ★ ★ ★ ★ ★ ★ ★ ★ ★ ★ ★ ★

London Gatwick
West Sussex. (0293) 503843. Busy airport with all types of aircraft, including light planes. 240-metre (800ft) viewing gallery gives a close-up of aircraft movements. *Open Apr-Oct 08.00-19.00 Mon-Sun; Nov-Mar 09.00-16.00 Mon-Sun; weather permitting.* Charge.

London Heathrow
Heathrow, Middx. 081-759 4321. From the viewing terrace see the planes land and take off. There's at least one a minute! Telescopes and refreshments. *Open 09.00-½ hr before dusk; all year.* Free.

★ *Arts* ★ ★ ★ ★ ★ ★ ★ ★ ★ ★ ★ ★ ★ ★ ★

Royal National Theatre   **5 A4**
South Bank SE1. 071-928 2252. Gives you a glimpse of the hard work and effort which goes into making the magic of the stage. A chance to see the prop stores, costume room and workshops. *Young children must be accompanied. To arrange tours phone or write to the above address. Tours last approximately 1 hour and take place at 10.15, 12.30 & 17.30 Mon-Sat.* Charge.

Royal Opera House, Covent Garden   **4 F2**
Bow St WC2. 071-240 1200. Visit workshops, dressing rooms, rehearsal rooms and the incredible wardrobe. *Young children must be accompanied. Essential to pre-book. Groups must be a minimum of 16 and maximum of 25. To arrange tours phone or write to the above address.* Charge.

Royal Shakespeare Company   **2 E6**
Barbican EC2. 071-628 3351 ex 7124. A tour backstage of the London home of the famous RSC including costume,

scenery and prop departments. *Young children must be accompanied. Tours run daily at 12.00 and 17.15. To arrange a tour advance booking is necessary; phone the RSC stating preferred dates and times. Groups must be a minimum of 8 and maximum of 30.* Charge.

Sadler's Wells Theatre 2 C4
Rosebery Ave EC1. 071-278 6563. Find out the history of Sadler's Wells and how it works today. A must for ballet lovers. Tours are arranged to fit the needs of the individual. *Young children must be accompanied. To arrange tours write to Backstage Tours (above address).* Charge.

★ *Auctioneers* ★ ★ ★ ★ ★ ★ ★ ★ ★ ★ ★ ★

Sotheby's 4 C3
34 New Bond St W1. 071-493 8080. Sotheby's is the world-famous auction house. There are auctions *Mon-Fri* and you can view the works of art in their 'lots'. *Advisable to visit in very small groups and definitely not suitable for young children. Open 09.00-16.30 Mon-Fri.* Free.

★ *Business and Finance* ★ ★ ★ ★ ★ ★ ★

Bank of England 5 E2
Threadneedle St EC2. 071-601 4444. Museum of the Bank of England (see *Museums & Galleries* on page 48) with exhibits relating to its history together with a video explaining the work of the bank today (aimed at 13+). *Open Apr Sep 10.00-17.00 Mon-Fri, 11.00-17.00 Sun; Oct-Mar 10.00-17.00 Mon-Fri.* Free.

★ *Farms* ★ ★ ★ ★ ★ ★ ★ ★ ★ ★ ★ ★ ★ ★

Surrey Docks Farm
Rotherhithe St SE16. 071-231 1010. Goats, pigs, donkeys, ducks, geese and hens. A blacksmith on site to demonstrate traditional skills. Educational schemes for school or group visits. *Open 10.00-13.00 & 14.00-17.00 Tue-Sun. Closed Mon & Fri in school hols. Phone for details.*

Stepping Stones Farm
Stepney Way E1. 071-790 8204. If you time it right you might be able to milk a goat or even watch a calf being born. A good way to learn the part farm animals play in our lives. *Book in advance. To arrange tours write or phone (above address) stating preferred dates and times. Young children must be accompanied. Open 09.00-18.00 Tue-Sun. Closed Mon.* Free (voluntary donation).

★ *Fire Stations* ★ ★ ★ ★ ★ ★ ★ ★ ★ ★ ★

Be right on the spot when the siren goes. For permission to visit your local fire station write to the PR Department, London Fire Brigade HQ, 8 Albert Embankment SE1 or telephone 071-582 3811. They will give you the number of your local fire station. *Only for children of 12 years and above.* Free.

★ *Glass Blowing* ★ ★ ★ ★ ★ ★ ★ ★ ★ ★ ★

The Glasshouse   **2 D2**
21 St Alban's Place, Islington N1. 071-359 8162. A mini glass factory and gallery. Watch glass being blown in the workshop from the viewing gallery during normal shop hours. *No organised tours. Open 11.00-18.00 Tue-Fri, 11.00-17.00 Sat.* Free.

London Glass-blowing Workshop
109 Rotherhithe St SE16. 071-237 0394. One of the longest-established studios in Britain, famous worldwide for innovative use of swirling, iridescent colour. *No organised tours but visitors welcome 10.00-18.00 Mon-Fri and by appointment Sat & Sun.*

★ *Law* ★ ★ ★ ★ ★ ★ ★ ★ ★ ★ ★ ★ ★ ★ ★

Inns of Court
Lincoln's Inn, Lincoln's Inn Fields WC2 (**5 A2**) 071-405 1393. Gray's Inn, Gray's Inn Rd WC1 (**5 B1**) 071-405 8164.

Inner Temple, King's Bench Walk EC4 (**5 B3**) 071-353 8462.
Middle Temple, Middle Temple Lane EC4 (**5 B3**) 071-353
4355.
The heart of the English legal system, where lawyers and
barristers go about their duties dressed in traditional wigs
and gowns. Some of the buildings date back to medieval
times and many famous people including Oliver Cromwell
and John Donne have studied here. *Phone or write for
admission details.*

Old Bailey   5 C2
Old Bailey EC4. 071-248 3277. The Old Bailey is on the site
of the Old Newgate prison; notice the statue of Justice on
top of the dome as you walk in. Trials in the Central Criminal
Court can be watched from the public galleries. Worth going
to see the wigs and robes worn by the judges and barristers. One of the most famous trials held here was that of
Peter Sutcliffe, the 'Yorkshire Ripper'. Tape recorders and
cameras are not permitted. *Minimum age 14. Children up to
age 16 must be accompanied by an adult. Open 10.30-13.00
& 14.00-16.00 Mon-Fri. Closed Bank hols.* Free.

★ *Music* ★ ★ ★ ★ ★ ★ ★ ★ ★ ★ ★ ★ ★ ★ ★

Boosey & Hawkes
Deansbrook Rd, Edgware, Middx. 081-952 7711. A tour
round the Boosey & Hawkes musical instrument factory
shows how a flat piece of brass is transformed into a shiny,
tuneful instrument. They specialise in brass pieces – the
horn, trumpet, trombone and tuba, and also flutes. *Write
well in advance to arrange tours. Tours at 10.00 & 14.00
Wed. Minimum age 11.* Charge (includes refreshments).

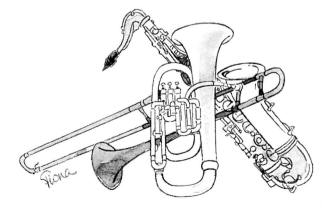

Royal Philharmonic Orchestra   **4 G1**
16 Clerkenwell Green EC1. 071-608 2381. Rehearsal seats available to members of the RPO Club or concert ticket holders only. *Minimum age 10. To attend a rehearsal individuals should write several weeks in advance.* Free.

★ *Politics* ★ ★ ★ ★ ★ ★ ★ ★ ★ ★ ★ ★ ★ ★

Houses of Parliament   **4 F5**
W1. 071-219 4272. To attend a debate in the House of Commons *apply to your local MP in writing*, or *queue at the St Stephen's entrance* (long queues in *summer*). Tours of Westminster Hall and Palace of Westminster also *by application to your local MP*. Free.

★ *Postal Services* ★ ★ ★ ★ ★ ★ ★ ★ ★ ★

Several of the large central offices offer conducted tours. At each place you can see sorting, postal machinery and the Post Office underground railway. *Minimum age 12. In each case write in advance to the Postmaster Controller. Mark envelope 'Visits'.*

King Edward Building   **5 D2**
King Edward St EC1. 071-239 5188. Concerned with London and overseas letter post; underground railway which carries thousands of sacks of mail a day. Tours *10.30 & 14.30 Mon, Wed & Thur. Groups of 22. Minimum age 10.* Free.

Mount Pleasant   **2 C5**
Farringdon Road EC1. 071-239 2191. Biggest sorting office in the country; underground railway. Tours *Jan-Nov. Groups of no more than 30. Book ten days in advance.* Free.

★ *Schools* ★ ★ ★ ★ ★ ★ ★ ★ ★ ★ ★ ★ ★ ★

Harrow School
15 London Rd, Harrow-on-the-Hill, Middx. 081-422 2303. Prime ministers, writers, poets and philanthropists are all among the former pupils of Harrow including Robert Peel, the 18th-century Prime Minister, Sheridan, the dramatist, the novelist Anthony Trollope, Lord Byron, the poet, and Winston Churchill. A lively and interesting tour around the school and grounds. *To arrange tours, phone or write to Harrow School Tours (above address) stating preferred times and dates. Tours Mon-Sat during term time and school hols.* Charge.

★ *Sport* ★ ★ ★ ★ ★ ★ ★ ★ ★ ★ ★ ★ ★ ★ ★

Lord's Cricket Ground
St John's Wood Rd NW8. 071-266 3825. Tours include the Long Room, the MCC Museum, the real tennis court, the mound stand and the indoor school. *Tours 12.00 & 14.00 Mon-Sun, plus 10.00 on a match day. Phone for availability.* Charge.

Twickenham Rugby Football Ground
Whitton Rd, Twickenham, Middx. 081-892 8161. Centre of the rugby world. Tour kicks off with a *15-minute* scene-setting video. You will be treated to the sights only the most privileged guests enjoy. *Tours by arrangement only. Write to the above address.* Charge.

Wembley Stadium
Empire Way, Wembley, Middx. 081-902 8833. 'The Wembley Stadium Tour' takes you from the Control Room, the nerve centre which controls every event at the stadium from sporting to pop concerts, through the changing rooms, up to the royal box and round the ground on the 'WembleyLand Train. In the cinema see a video of great moments from the stadium's past, plus clips of more recent pop concerts. Tours *summer 10.00-16.00 Mon-Sun; winter 10.00-15.00 Mon-Sun.* Charge.

Wimbledon Lawn Tennis Museum
All England Club, Church Rd SW19. 081-946 6131. The history of lawn tennis with an excellent video showing films of great matches. You are even allowed to peek into the famous Centre Court. *Open 10.30-17.00 Tue-Sat, 14.00-17.00 Sun. Closed Mon.* Charge.

★ *Telephone Services* ★ ★ ★ ★ ★ ★ ★ ★

Story of Telecommunications   5 C3
145 Queen Victoria St EC4. 071-248 7444. Displays history of telecommunications, highlighting the best of present-day design and offering a glimpse of the future. You'll find there's a lot more to telecommunications than meets the eye. *Not suitable for young children. Open 10.00-17.00 Mon-Fri. Closed Bank hols.* Free.

★ Out of Doors

★ *Parks & Gardens* ★ ★ ★ ★ ★ ★ ★ ★ ★ ★

London has over 80 parks within 7 miles of its centre, more than almost any other city in the world. They are all that remain of early London's surrounding countryside. The ten royal parks were originally the grounds of royal homes or palaces and are still the property of the crown.

We have listed most of the famous royal parks, some of the less well-known local parks plus a few close to London. Each park has an individual character – you may prefer the wild expanses of Richmond to civilised Green Park. For a pleasant rural walk in the heart of London walk through St James's Park, past Buckingham Palace into Green Park and from there into Hyde Park. Read about each park before you head off and then you'll know whether to take swimming things, money for boats, a kite or a football. All parks are free but there are charges for some individual facilities.

Alexandra Park & Palace N22

081-365 2121. An enormous park with a superb view of the London skyline. Attractions include a boating lake, pitch and putt, animal enclosure, parkland walk, children's playground, garden centre, conservation area, ski slope and ice-rink. Alexandra Palace is now an exhibition centre and leisure venue. *Open 24 hours Mon-Sun.*

Avery Hill SE9

Bexley Rd SE9. 081-850 2666. The Winter Garden is a second, smaller Kew. A botanist's paradise full of tropical and sub-tropical Asian and Australasian plants. Greenhouses *open 10.00-16.00 Mon-Thur, 10.00-15.00 Fri, 10.00-18.30 Sat & Sun (to 17.00 in winter).* Park *open 08.00-21.00 (or dusk) Mon-Sun.*

Battersea Park SW11   **6 F5**

081-871 7530. A great riverside park with lots going on: boating lake, deer park, children's zoo and a botanical wild flower garden. Pony rides for children in *summer* and an Easter Show (see *Calendar* on page 17). *Open dawn-dusk Mon-Sun.* Playing fields, athletics track and tennis courts (081-871 6359 for details) *open 08.00-dusk Mon-Sun.*

Blackheath SE3
081-854 8888. Large open common, ideal for kite-flying. Plenty of room for soccer and cricket and you can sail model boats on the Prince of Wales pond. Funfairs at *Easter, spring and late summer Bank hols.* Some of the runners who compete in the London Marathon, held every *spring,* start from here. *Open 24 hours Mon-Sun.*

Crystal Palace Park SE20
081-778 7148. Named after the Great Exhibition building which was moved here from Hyde Park. Now a National Youth & Sports Centre with an Olympic swimming pool and modern sports stadium in a large open park. Plenty of space for ball games, biking and kite-flying. Activities for children – a playpark, farmyard, miniature railway track, shire horse cart rides, ranger guided walks, circular maze, mini fair and a wonderful boating and fishing lake. The four islands in the lake are 'colonised' by 20 life-sized replicas of the dinosaur and other early animals. Annual events include classic car shows, firework displays and a classical concert season *Jul/Aug.* Phone for details. *Open 08.00-½ hr before dusk Mon-Sun.*

Dulwich Park SE21
081-693 5737. A favourite garden of the late Queen Mary, wife of George V, and you can see why when all the rhododendrons are out. Boating lake and tennis. Refreshments in the Rose Garden. *Open summer 08.00-21.00 Mon-Sun; winter 08.00-16.30 Mon-Sun.*

Epping Forest, Essex
2436 hectares (6000 acres) of natural woodland, 6 miles long and 2 miles wide stretching from Chingford to Epping. Opened to the public in 1878, it was dedicated to the public forever. Many hornbeam, oak, ash, maple, beech and birch trees; it also offers a superb variety of all kinds of natural life – there are so many grey squirrels that they have become a problem. High Beech is a popular spot and there are large areas to ramble through where you can get thoroughly lost, or even stumble upon the remains of the two ancient British camps at least 2000 years old – Loughton Camp and Amersbury Banks. *Open 24 hours Mon-Sun.*

Green Park SW1   4 C5
071-930 1793. A welcome green space in the heart of London. An abundance of lime, plane and hawthorn trees makes this a shady place to stroll and the expansive lawns make ideal picnic spots. *Open dawn-dusk Mon-Sun.*

Greenwich Park SE10
081-858 2608. A royal park of 97 hectares (200 acres) with pleasant avenues lined with chestnut trees sloping down to

the Thames; contains the Old Royal Observatory and its pleasant garden, acres of wooded deer park and Bronze Age tumuli. *Open summer 07.00 (for traffic, 05.00 for pedestrians)-dusk Mon-Sun; winter 07.00-18.00 (or dusk) Mon-Sun.*

Hampstead Heath NW3

071-485 4491 (Parliament Hill); 081-455 5183 (Golders Hill Park). High, open and hilly park and woods, excellent for walking. Includes Parliament Hill, Golders Hill (containing a fine English town garden) and Kenwood. Plenty of room here to escape the crowds. Masses of facilities: 10 tennis courts, Olympic track, orienteering, cricket, football, rugby, rounders, an adventure playground and one o'clock club. Also swimming in Hampstead Ponds: 081-348 1033 (Kenwood Ladies Pond), 071-485 3873 (Parliament Hill Lido), a children's zoo at Golders Hill and lots to see for the keen ornithologist (over 100 species of birds have been sighted here). *Open 24 hours Mon-Sun.* Golders Hill *open dawn-dusk Mon-Sun.*

Hampton Court & Bushy Park, Surrey

081-781 9750. Hampton is the formal park of the great Tudor palace with superb flower gardens and the famous maze. Its amazing gardens were planned to rival Versailles. Bushy Park has natural parkland, an artificial plantation, watercourses and ornamental ponds, and a magnificent chestnut-lined avenue. Large herd of deer. Play area. *Open 07.00-dusk Mon-Sun.*

Holland Park W8   3 A5

071-602 9483. Behind Kensington High Street are secluded lawns and gardens with peacocks, once the private garden of Holland House. Also iris and rose gardens, yucca lawn, Japanese garden and the Orangery. On the north side is a woodland containing 3000 species of rare British trees and plants, full of birds – exotic species include Muscovy ducks and Polish bantams. Adventure playground and one o'clock club, tennis courts, golf and cricket nets, football and cricket pitches, squash courts. Open-air theatre *May-Aug.* Restaurant. Park *open summer 07.30-sunset Mon-Sun; winter 07.30-dusk Mon-Sun.* Restaurant looks out onto Flower Garden which is illuminated at night.

Hyde Park W1   3 F4

071-298 2100. A royal park since 1536, it was once part of the forest reserved by Henry VIII for hunting. In the Domesday Book it was thick forest and well-populated with deer, boar and wild bulls. Hyde Park now has 140 hectares (344 acres) of parkland, walks, Rotten Row for horse riders and the Serpentine – a fine lake for boating and swimming (the Lido). Also putting green and four tennis courts. Park *open 05.00-24.00 Mon-Sun.* The Lido *open Jun-Sep 10.00-dusk Mon-Sun.* Charge for swimming.

Kensington Gardens W8   **3 D4**
071-298 2117. A formal and elegant addition to Hyde Park,
containing William III's lovely Kensington Palace, Queen
Anne's Orangery, the peaceful Sunken Garden and the
Round Pond which is always busy with model sailing boats.
Good children's playground with the Elfin Oak – carved with
lots of birds and animals. The swings here were given by
J.M. Barrie, the author of *Peter Pan*, who is celebrated with
a statue of the character. *Open dawn-dusk Mon-Sun.*

Peter Pan

Primrose Hill NW8   **1 B2**
071-486 7905. A minor royal park – a simple grassy hill
giving a fine view over London. Children's play areas.
Puppet shows in *summer. Open 24 hours Mon-Sun.*

Regent's Park NW1   **1 C4**
071-486 7905. Originally part of Henry VIII's great hunting
forest in the 16th century. Contains the famous London Zoo

and aviary, the Regent's Canal, a great boating lake with 30 species of bird, a bandstand and an open-air theatre in *summer*. Plus three children's playgrounds, tennis courts, cricket, baseball, football pitches. Puppet shows *Jul-Aug. Open 05.00 (or dawn)-dusk Mon-Sun.*

Richmond Park, Surrey

081-948 3209. A royal park first enclosed by Charles I in 1637. Beautiful parkland with plenty of room to run around in. Over 400 fallow deer roam around the park and foxes, weasels and the occasional badger can also be seen. Golf, riding, polo and fishing (permit required). *Open 07.00 (07.30 in winter)-½ hr before dusk Mon-Sun.*

Royal Botanic Gardens, Kew

Kew Rd, Richmond, Surrey. 081-940 1171. Superb botanical gardens stocked with thousands of flowers and trees. There's the Princess of Wales Conservatory for orchids, palms, ferns, cacti and water lilies the size of mattresses, the magnificent curved glass Palm House and the Temperate House for more exotic plants and trees. Beneath the Palm House there is a Marine Display which has examples of flowering marine plants and coral reef. Cafeteria and gift shop in the Orangery. *1-hour* tours available from the Victoria Gate Visitor Centre. *Groups should book in advance by phoning the Guided Tours Organiser on 081-332 5623. Gardens open 09.30, closing times vary according to season.* Charge.

St James's Park SW1   4 E5

071-930 1793. This, the oldest royal park, was acquired in 1532 by Henry VIII and completely redesigned by Charles II, imitating Versailles as much as possible. An attractive park with fine promenades and walks and a romantic Chinese-style lake, bridge and weeping willows. The bird sanctuary on Duck Island has some magnificent pelicans and over 20 species of duck and goose. The pelicans were originally given to Charles II for the royal menagerie by a Russian ambassador. On the north bank there are picture tiles to help identify the different species. Playground with sand-pit and swings. Refreshments at the Cake House. *Open dawn-dusk Mon-Sun.*

Wimbledon Common

081-788 7655. Wild woodland, open heath and several ponds. Golf course, horse riding and playing fields here. Famous old 19th-century windmill with a museum inside and tea rooms outside. Museum *open in summer and on fine weekends. Phone for opening times.* Park *open 24 hours Mon-Sun.* Tea rooms *open 09.30-17.30 Mon-Sun.*

ANIMAL AND BIRD ENCLOSURES IN PARKS ▰▰▰▰▰

They are open from *dawn-dusk Mon-Sun,* unless otherwise stated, and all are free.

Battersea Park SW11   **6 G5**
081-871 7540. Zoo with small collection of animals. Reptile house, wide variety of primates, otter, meerkat and mongoose enclosures, flamingoes, ponies and donkeys, deer, wallabies, rheas. *Open Easter-Oct 11.00-18.00 Mon-Sun; Nov-Mar 11.00-15.00 Sat & Sun only.*

Brockwell Park SE24
071-926 0105. Small collection of birds including doves, canaries, finches, budgerigars and chickens.

Clissold Park N16
081-800 1021. Fallow deer, red-neck terrapins, guinea pigs, tropical birds, as well as a peacock and a collection of water-fowl.

Crystal Palace SE20
081-778 7148. Farm with shire horses, cows, pigs, rabbits, chickens, donkeys, penguins, otters, goats, sheep and ponies. Shire horse cart rides round the park for children. *Open 11.00-17.00 Mon-Sun.*

Golders Hill Park NW11
081-455 5183. Fallow deer, pygmy goats, wallabies and black-buck. Birds include pheasants, cranes, flamingoes and rheas.

Hainault Forest, Essex
081-500 3106. Ponies, donkeys, cows, a goat, a rabbit house and pigs. Also a small collection of domestic and wild fowl, including peacocks and guinea fowl.

Holland Park W8   **3 A5**
071-602 9483. Collection of birds, including peacocks, ban-tams, Muscovy ducks and peafowl.

London Butterfly House
Syon Park, Brentford, Middx. 081-560 7272. A greenhouse full of tropical and temperate butterflies; if you're very lucky you'll witness the emergence of a butterfly as it struggles from its pupal case. There is also an additional gallery featuring a variety of insects and bizarre invertebrates. *Open Apr-Oct 10.00-17.00 Mon-Sun; Nov-Mar 10.00-15.30 Mon-Sun.* Charge.

Maryon Wilson Park SE7
081-854 4902. Ponies, goats, ducks, turkeys, peafowl, chin-cillas, guinea pigs, fallow deer and Jacob sheep plus rabbits and chickens.

Plashet Park E6
081-503 5994. A mini-zoo with a collection of small animals. Tropical aviary and butterfly house. *Open summer 10.00-17.00 Mon-Sun; winter 10.00-16.00 Mon-Sun.*

Victoria Park E2
081-985 1957. A small enclosure on the eastern side of the park with fallow deer and pygmy goats. A wide variety of wild birds can be seen on the other side of the park.

MUSIC IN THE PARKS

On *summer afternoons* you can listen to military and brass bands in Hyde Park (**4 B4**), Regent's Park (**1 B5**) and St James's Park (**4 E5**). Check *Time Out* for details.

★ *Cemeteries* ★ ★ ★ ★ ★ ★ ★ ★ ★ ★ ★ ★ ★

Some children find cemeteries fascinating rather than morbid or frightening and many of London's older cemeteries are wonderful to explore.

Bunhill Burial Fields   **2 F5**
Bunhill Fields EC1 (originally Bone Hill). A well-known burial site even before the 1500s, when St Paul's began to send old bones from the churchyard as space was needed to bury people. You can still see the graves of Daniel Defoe, who wrote *Robinson Crusoe,* and William Blake, the poet and painter.

Highgate Cemetery
Swain's Lane N6. 081-340 1834. Probably the most interesting of the cemeteries and filled with famous 'residents' – Karl Marx, founder of modern communism, prize fighter Tom Sayers and poet Christina Rossetti to name but a few. East cemetery *Apr-Oct 10.00-17.00 Mon-Fri, 11.00-17.00 Sat & Sun; Nov-Mar 10.00-16.00 Mon-Fri, 11.00-16.00 Sat & Sun.* West cemetery guided tours only *Apr-Oct 12.00, 14.00 & 16.00 Mon-Fri, on the hour between 11.00-16.00 Sat & Sun; Nov & Mar 12.00, 14.00 & 15.00 Mon-Fri, on the hour between 11.00-15.00 Sat & Sun. No weekday tours Dec-Feb. Special tours for groups of 10 or more must be arranged by appointment.*

★ *Fairs* ★ ★ ★ ★ ★ ★ ★ ★ ★ ★ ★ ★ ★ ★ ★

There are over 200 fairs a week held in England during the *summer;* the following is a selection of some in London.

Holiday Fairs
Alexandra Park, Blackheath, Hampstead Heath and Wormwood Scrubs have fairs every major holiday *(Easter, spring and summer Bank hols).*

Other Occasional Fairs
Clapham Common *(mid Apr)*, Crystal Palace *(early May & Aug)*, Tooting Bec Common *(early May)*, Victoria Park *(early May)*.

★ *Farms* ★ ★ ★ ★ ★ ★ ★ ★ ★ ★ ★ ★ ★ ★

There are several farms which are open to visitors in and around London. In London itself there are small city farms which welcome visits from families and school groups and often like help with feeding, grooming and mucking out. Outside London you can visit large working farms which organise open days and farm trails. If you're going in a group it's wise to phone and give advance warning.

College Farm
Fitzalan Rd N3. 081-349 0690. Small children's farm with cows, goats, pigs, sheep and shire horses. Special events *on first Sun of month* – craft stalls, donkey rides, bouncy castle. *Open 10.00-18.00 Mon-Sun.* Charge.

Freightliners Farm
Entrance: Sheringham Rd N7. 071-609 0467. Small, busy city farm with cows and calves, sheep, goats and kids, ducks, pigs, geese, bees and chickens. Lots of opportunities to get involved with the animals. Café and farmshop. Goslings playgroup *Thur mornings. Phone for times of tours. Groups must phone in advance. Open 09.00-13.00 & 14.00-17.00 Tue-Sun. Closed Mon.* Free (voluntary donation).

Hackney City Farm
1a Goldsmith's Row, off Hackney Rd E2. 071-729 6381. The farm is stocked with sheep, goats, pigs, calves, rabbits, ducks and bees. Pottery, spinning and weaving classes. Offers an 'animal loan scheme' where schools can borrow rabbits and guinea pigs for children to learn about animals first hand. Ecological pond and wildflower areas, beekeeping, butterfly tunnel. *Open 10.00-16.30 Tue-Sun. Closed Mon.* Free.

Mudchute Farm
Pier St E14. 071-515 5901. More like the real thing than most city farms, because it has grassland spreading over the Mudchute's 13 hectares (32 acres). Locals set it up in 1977 and several full-time staff are required to look after the cattle, ponies, sheep, goats, pigs, poultry, rabbits and bees. All the animals can be observed and most handled. There is also a riding school with a qualified teacher. Nature study centre. Café. *Open 09.00-17.00 Mon-Sun.* Free.

Spitalfields Farm
Weaver Street, behind Thomas Buxton Junior School, Buxton St E1. 071-247 8762. There are pigs, goats, sheep, poultry, cattle, rabbits, donkeys. Learn to feed, muck out, milk and bed down the animals. Pony rides and local history horse cart tours. Free pottery, spinning and weaving

classes. *Open 09.00-18.00 Tue-Sun. Closed Mon.* Free (voluntary donation).

Stepping Stones Farm

Stepney Way E1. 071-790 8204. Local volunteers are invited to help out on all sorts of jobs, but everyone is welcome to visit this 6 acre urban farm in the East End. Activities vary with the seasons but the livestock population usually includes pigs, goats, cows, sheep, ducks, geese, rabbits and donkeys. Wildlife pond. Picnic garden. Produce shop. *Advisable to phone in advance. Open 09.30-18.00 Tue-Sun. Closed Mon.* Free (voluntary donation).

Surrey Docks Farm

Rotherhithe St SE16. 071-231 1010. Goats, pigs, donkeys, ducks, geese and hens mill about together on this small site. Also there's a small orchard, vegetable garden, herb garden, wild area, duck pond and riverside walk. A blacksmith is on site to demonstrate traditional skills. There are educational schemes for school or group visits, or you can just wander round. The farm shop sells yoghurt, honey, cheese, eggs and organic vegetables in *summer*. Tea cakes in the café *at weekends. Open 10.00-13.00 & 14.00-17.00 Tue-Sun. Closed Mon & Fri in school hols.* Free.

Vauxhall City Farm

Tyers Street SE11. 071-582 4204. Tours to visit the pigs, goats, sheep and rabbits. Pony and donkey rides. *Open 10.30-17.00 Tue-Thur, Sat & Sun.* Charge (for tours only).

★ *Nature Reserves & Trails* ★ ★ ★ ★ ★ ★

Nature Conservancy Council
Northminster House, Peterborough. (0733) 340345.
Regional offices will supply a list of reserves and
leaflets about individual reserves in Great Britain.

Camley Street Natural Park　　　　　　　　　　**1 G3**

12 Camley St NW1. 071-833 2311. A park which has been created in a former coal drop on the Grand Union Canal to provide a wildlife refuge and a place to enjoy nature in the city. Has a Visitor Centre which includes a classroom. *Phone in advance if visiting in a group. Open Apr-Oct 09.00-17.00 Mon-Thur, 11.00-17.00 Sat & Sun; Nov-Mar 09.00-17.00 Mon-Thur, 10.00-16.00 Sat & Sun; Summer hols open 10.00-18.00 Mon-Thur, 11.00-17.00 Sat & Sun.* Free (voluntary donation).

East Ham Nature Reserve

Norman Rd E6. 081-470 4525. A nature reserve in the heart

of East London's largest churchyard. Follow the nature trail. See pheasants and butterflies. Special activities *during school hols. Open 09.00-17.00 (dusk in winter) Mon-Sun.* Visitor Centre *open 14.00-17.00 Sat & Sun. Free.*

Horniman Gardens
London Rd, Forest Hill SE23. 081-699 8924. Three separate walks: the Coach Trail, the Dutch Barn Trail and the Railway Trail which follows the track of the old Crystal Palace high level railway line. Two guides to the trails are available from the Park Manager's office and the Horniman Museum for a nominal fee. Museum *open 10.30-18.00 Mon-Sat, 14.00-18.00 Sun.* Garden *closed at dusk. Free.*

Trent Park
Barnet, Herts. 081-449 8706. A huge park with a popular nature trail that you can do on your own or with a ranger to guide you. If desired, a programme of events can be drawn up for both children and adults. They also offer slide shows a week before the trail and then question and answer sessions on the day of the trail. Wildlife club meets *once a fortnight.* Pets Corner with goats, sheep, rabbits etc. Also special three-quarter mile woodland trail for the blind and partially-sighted. Watergarden and two lakes. *Open 07.30-dusk Mon-Sun. Free.*

★ *Playgrounds & Playcentres* ★ ★ ★ ★ ★

Most parks have playgrounds of some sort. The following are organisations which run playgrounds and will help you find the best one near you.

PLAYGROUNDS

Adventure Playgrounds
Community-based playgrounds, run by playworkers, who organise activities indoors and out for school-age children. Children are usually free to build dens for example, using old timber and junk. For more information contact Playlink, 279 Whitechapel Rd E1. 071-377 0314. *Open after school, at weekends & during school hols. Free.*

Conventional Playgrounds
Provided by borough councils in most local parks. They usually have tarmac surfaces with swings, roundabouts, slides, see-saws, climbing frames and rocking horses. Some of this equipment is potentially dangerous for small children and newer, safer playgrounds now have swings made of rubber tyres, built-up slides made of durable plastic and wood chip surrounds instead of tarmac or concrete. *Open 08.00-19.00 (or dusk) Mon-Sun. Free.*

Handicapped Adventure Playground Association
Fulham Palace, Bishops Ave SW6. 071-736 4443. The association runs five playgrounds for the disabled in London and provides information about its services as well as play ideas for disabled children. Also advisory service which gives help to those wishing to set up their own playground.

One O'Clock Clubs
Enclosed area in some parks, exclusively for children under 5. Each club has a building for indoor play (painting, modelling etc) and an outdoor enclosure with climbing frames, water and sand. Playworkers supervise activities but a parent or guardian is expected to stay on the premises. Informal and friendly. To find your nearest club, contact the local borough council. *Open 13.00-16.30 Mon-Fri.* Free.

PLAYPARKS

Intended for children of 5-15 years, the aim is towards free play with structures for climbing, swinging etc and playworkers to supervise. You'll find them in Alexandra Park, Battersea Park, Crystal Palace Park, Holland Park and on Hampstead Heath (Parliament Hill Fields). Contact the local borough council for information. *Open summer 11.30-20.00 Mon-Sun.* Free.

★ *Walks* ★ ★ ★ ★ ★ ★ ★ ★ ★ ★ ★ ★ ★ ★

Canal walks
Contact Inland Waterways Association, 114 Regent's Park Rd NW1 (071-586 2556) for full details.
Here are a few suggestions:
Salmon Lane Lock to Camden Town (about 6 miles)
Camden Town to Little Venice (2½ miles)
Little Venice to Willesden Junction (over 3 miles)
Willesden Junction to Bull's Bridge, Southall (9½ miles)
Brentford Lock to Hayes (5 miles)
Hayes to Uxbridge (over 5 miles)

London walks
PO Box 1708, London NW6. 071-624 3978. Meet at various tube stations for stimulating walks through London lasting *1½-2 hours*. More than 60 walks including *Dickens' London*, *Ghosts of the City* and *Jack the Ripper haunts*. *Phone for details*. Charge.

Silver Jubilee Walkway
London Tourist Board & Convention Bureau, Tourist Information Centre, Victoria Station Forecourt SW1. Buy a booklet from the London Tourist Board or follow the paving stones marked with Jubilee crowns. This pedestrian trail takes you across London from Leicester Square to Tower Hill.

★ *Zoos & Aquaria* ★ ★ ★ ★ ★ ★ ★ ★ ★ ★

London Aquarium 1 C3
Regent's Park NW1. 071-722 3333. Marine and Tropical Halls. Excellently lit and displayed. A well-stocked aquarium of both sea and freshwater fish and amphibians from European and tropical waters. Particularly notable are the fine sea fish, the octopuses and stingrays. Combined entry with London Zoo. *Open Mar-Oct 10.00-17.30 Mon-Sun; Nov-Feb 10.00-dusk Mon-Sun. Closed Xmas Day.* Charge (includes admittance to London Zoo).

London Zoo 1 C3
Regent's Park NW1. 071-722 3333. This famous zoo has one of the largest collections of animals in the world. Aviary designed by Lord Snowdon and 'Moonlight World' where day and night are reversed and rarely seen nocturnal animals are kept awake during the day. There's also 'Lifewatch' for children. Membership allows you free entry to London Zoo, plus a magazine, discounts and special events. Tours arranged for school parties. Restaurant, café or bring your own picnic and eat in the grounds. Combined entry with London Aquarium. *Open Mar-Oct 10.00-17.30 Mon-Sun; Nov-Feb 10.00-dusk Mon-Sun. Closed Xmas Day.* Charge (includes admittance to London Aquarium).

★ Fun Days Out

Beaulieu

85 miles SW

Brockenhurst, Hants. (0590) 612345. A host of activities on offer here: high level monorail, radio-controlled cars to be raced, miniature bike and car track. The main attraction is the fantastic National Motor Museum. Recall the first hundred years of motoring in 'Wheels – The Legend of the Motor Car' – an exhibition where sound and movement recreate the trials endured by early motorists. Also take part in 'The Vauxhall Driving Experience' – a simulated ride through the ages experiencing motoring in the 1920s to modern rally driving. *Open May-Sep 10.00-18.00 Mon-Sun; Oct-Apr 10.00-17.00 Mon-Sun. Closed Xmas Day.* Charge.

Bekonscot Model Village

23 miles NW

Warwick Rd, Beaconsfield, Bucks. (0494) 672919. The oldest model village in the world, Bekonscot is an escape into rural England in the 1930s. Accountant Roland Callingham built the model village in a field opposite his home, choosing the name as a mixture of Beaconsfield where he was living and Ascot, his former home. A raised viewing platform offers a bird's eye view of the miniature world of shops, streets and inhabitants, but the real home pride of Bekonscot is the model (gauge 1) railway which travels round the village. Picnic facilities and playground. *Open Mar-Oct 10.00-17.00 Mon-Sun.* Charge.

Birdworld & Underwater World

30 miles SW

Holt Pound, Farnham, Surrey. (0420) 22140. Situated on the edge of Alice Holt Forest, there are beautiful gardens here which make the perfect home for a huge variety of birds from the tiny humming bird to the huge ostrich. Watch the pelicans catch fish in their beaks or feeding time at Penguin Island. There are good, well laid-out trails, the most popular of which is Seashore Walk, an area re-created as a seashore complete with waves, the wreck of a fishing boat and many kinds of seabird.

Underwater World is next door, with a large indoor aquarium full of an amazing array of colourful tropical fish. They can be visited separately or together. There's also a children's farm, a play area and café. *Open Apr-Aug 09.30-18.00 Mon-Sun; Sep 09.30-17.00 Mon-Sun; Oct-Mar 09.30-16.30 Mon-Sun.* Charge.

Bluebell Railway
46 miles S

Sheffield Park Station, nr Uckfield, East Sussex. (082572) 2370. 24-hour train information, bookings and enquiries (082572) 3777. An excellent outing with a difference. Opened in 1960, the first of the disused steam passenger lines to be restored to working order, the Bluebell Railway runs along a former British Railway branch line between Sheffield Park, New Coombe Bridge and the newly-opened Kingscote Station. Everything from the station to the signal boxes and adverts have been restored. You can also browse round the engine shed and take a closer look at the historic locomotives, coaches and wagons. *Open Apr-Sep 10.00-17.00 Sat & Sun; Oct-Mar 10.00-17.00 Sat & Sun. Phone for individual train times.* Charge.

Brighton Sea Life Centre
45 miles S

Marine Parade, Brighton, East Sussex. (0273) 6042334. Oldest public aquarium in Britain containing about 40 tanks of marine and freshwater fish. Watch the sharks and other fish swim above you in the Shark Tunnel. Restaurant. *Open summer 10.00-21.00 Mon-Sun; winter 10.00-17.00 Mon-Sun. Closed Xmas Day.* Charge.

Butlin's Southcoast World
60 miles SW

Bognor Regis, West Sussex. (0243) 822445. All the fun of the fair for a flat-price entrance fee. Family favourites like the dodgem cars and the carousel. Giant indoor adventure-land, sub-tropical waterworld, children's theatre shows and blockbuster movies. *Open Apr-Oct 10.00-21.30 Mon-Sun (last admission 17.00); Nov-Mar 10.00-21.30 Sat & Sun (last admission 16.00).* Charge.

Chessington World of Adventures
15 miles SW

Leatherhead Rd, Chessington, Surrey. (0372) 727227. Designed to give the whole family a great day out with everything from spine-tingling rides to rare wild animals. Entrance charge covers everything so you can have as many rides as you can fit into the day. Various 'worlds' occupy separate areas and are all distinctly different. Visit the Forbidden Kingdom, the Mystic East, Calamity Canyon,

Circus World and Toytown. A monorail travels high above the zoo animals. Theme park and circus *open mid Mar-Oct 10.00-17.00 Mon-Sun*. Zoo *open all year 10.00-16.00 Mon-Sun (last admission 15.00). Closed Xmas Day*. Charge.

Chislehurst Caves

12 miles SE

Old Hill, Chislehurst, Kent. 081-467 3264. A maze of chalk tunnels and caves, created in the stone ages and used ever since. Go on one of the eerie lamplight guided tours. They last *45-mins* and leave *every half hour*. On *Sun and Bank holidays* there is a *1½-hr* tour which leaves at *14.30*. The caves have been inhabited in the past by druids, the Romans and Londoners seeking shelter during the air raids of World War II. Listen out for the chilling stories of druid sacrifices and ghosts. Refreshments available. *Open 11.00-16.30 Mon-Sun*. Charge.

Cotswold Wildlife Park

75 miles W

Burford, Oxon. (099382) 3006. Set in 120 acres of gardens and parkland. Large and varied collection of animals can be seen in natural surroundings. Rhinos, zebras and ostrich roam in large paddocks bounded by unobtrusive moats. But some of the more dangerous species, like the leopards, are caged. Watch the penguins at feeding time. See tropical birds in the walled garden. Plenty for children to do, with an adventure playground and farmyard, where tame animals – pigs, lambs, goats, llamas, ducks and rabbits – can be stroked. There is a narrow gauge railway which operates in the park during *summer*. Special events such as demonstrations of birds of prey and car rallies. Restaurant, brass rubbing centre. Children can become Junior Friends of the Park for a small membership fee. *Open 10.00-18.00 (or dusk) Mon-Sun. Closed Xmas Day*. Charge.

Hatfield House

25 miles NE

Hatfield House, Hatfield, Herts. (07072) 62823. Elizabeth I spent most of her youth here (virtually a prisoner during the reign of her sister Mary Queen of Scots) and it was here she heard the news of her accession to the throne in 1558. You can see two portraits of Elizabeth as well as her hat, gloves and stockings (the first silk stocking worn in England) in the present house. Letters written by Mary Queen of Scots and Lord Burghley, Elizabeth's chief advisor, are on display in the library. National collection of British model soldiers housed here. Make sure you wander round the magnificent park and gardens. *Open Mar-mid Oct 12.00-16.00 Tue-Sat (for tours only), 13.30-17.00 Sun (for general public)*. Charge.

Thorpe Park
21 miles SW
Staines Rd, Chertsey, Surrey. (0932) 562633. A wonderful place for the whole family. Travel down a huge waterslide in an inflatable raft at Fantasy Reef, shoot the rapids down Thunder River, visit the pyramids of Egypt, travel on the Rocky Mountain Railway. Catch the ferry to Thorpe Farm. Enjoy jazz bands or cartoon comedy at Showtime. Those over 1 metre tall and under 12 years can join the Thorpe Park Rangers club (charge) which allows them half price admission for two years. All the rides are covered by the entrance fee, including repeat trips. *Open end Mar-Jun 10.00-17.00 Mon-Sun; Jul-Sep 10.00-18.00 Mon-Sun; Oct 10.00-17.00; (last admission 2 hours before closing time). Closed Nov-end Mar.* Charge (children under 1 metre tall free!).

Whipsnade Wild Animal Park
32 miles N
Dunstable, Beds. (0582) 872171. 600 acres of rolling parkland with over 3000 rare and exciting animals. See cheetahs, lions, tigers, elephants, rhinos and reptiles. Meet the farm animals, watch the sealions' splashtime or the birds of prey in flight. There is a Discovery Centre with hands-on displays, a miniature desert and wall-to-wall rainforests. Plus an adventure play centre and a narrow gauge steam railway. You can picnic in the grounds – take binoculars or use the telescopes provided. Go round the park in your own car or aboard the miniature motor coach train. *Open Apr-Oct 10.00-dusk Mon-Sun; Nov-Mar 10.00-16.00 Mon-Sun. Closed Xmas Day.* Charge.

Windsor Castle
20 miles W
Windsor, Berks. (0753) 868286. The castle was originally built by William the Conqueror and is the oldest and largest inhabited castle in the world. It covers about 5.3 hectares (13 acres) in total. A good time to visit is *11.00* for the spectacle of the Changing of The Guard. Inside are sumptuous state apartments, which are open to the public. St George's Hall and the Grand Reception Room were severely damaged by fire in November 1992. Visitors can still watch the renovations taking place through perspex screens. Make sure you see Queen Mary's Dolls' House, designed by the architect Sir Edward Lutyens. *Opening times depend on the movements of the royal family and*

Windsor Castle

ceremonial occasions, so check with the Castle Information Office. Charge.

Woburn Safari Park

44 miles NW

Woburn, Beds. (0525) 290407. Britain's largest drive-through wildlife park. A winding route takes you past tigers, bears, wolves, rhinos and mischievous monkeys! At the end of the Safari Trail you can see parrot and sealion shows. Adventure playground, boating lake, pets corner. Must have own car to drive through park. *Open mid Mar-Oct 10.00-17.00 Mon-Sun; Nov-mid Mar 11.00-15.00 Sat & Sun.* Charge.

★ Entertainment

Kidsline (071-222 8070) is a phone information service which provides details of entertainments in London. *Open 16.00-18.00 Mon-Fri in term time, 09.00-16.00 Mon-Fri in school hols.*

★ Theatre ★ ★ ★ ★ ★ ★ ★ ★ ★ ★ ★ ★ ★ ★

The following theatres put on children's shows regularly throughout the year. Phone for programme details, or see the weekly magazines *Time Out* or *What's On*. We have not included many of the touring theatres *but* look out to see if Oyly Cart, Quicksilver, the Pop Up Theatre, Whirligig and Soap Box are playing near you. They put on wonderful dramatic and musical productions that are specially written and produced for children.

Barbican   **5 D1**
Silk St EC2. 071-638 4141 ex 218. Box office 071-638 8891. Annual festival 'Summer in the City' for all the family in the *summer hols* with concerts, clowns, scavenger hunts and workshops. *Phone for details.*

Little Angel Marionette Theatre   **2 D2**
14 Dagmar Passage, off Cross St N1. 071-226 1787. London's only permanent puppet theatre, which presents an excellent variety of shows by their own company and visiting puppeteers. Shows usually based on traditional folk tales. Essential to book in advance. Regular performances *15.00 Sat & Sun* for older children and adults. Special show for the very young (3-6 year-olds) *11.00 Sat & Sun.* Extra shows during *half term and school hols.*

London Bubble
5 Elephant Lane SE16. 071-237 4434. The London Bubble is a mobile arts company. The summer tour travels through London's parks from *May-Sep* each year and in *spring* they do a community tour. Fun and definitely entertaining musicals, plays and cabaret plus a range of participatory theatre projects. *Phone for details.*

Lyric Theatre, Hammersmith
King St W6. 081-741 2311. Children's hour *11.00 Sat*. Lots of entertainment including plays, clowns, puppet shows, story-telling sessions, dance and music. Workshops. Children's portions in the café.

Molecule Theatre of Science   4 F2
12 Mercer St WC2. 071-379 5093. Touring theatre group for young people, performing exciting and inventive plays that aim to bridge the gap between science and drama. *Phone for London dates*.

Polka Children's Theatre
240 The Broadway SW19. 081-543 4888. Three hundred seat theatre built especially for children with plays, puppet shows and concerts; exhibitions of toys and puppets; children's workshop, adventure room, garden playground and café that caters for children (age 3 upwards). Full facilities for handicapped children including a loop system for deaf children. *Open 09.30-16.30 Tue-Fri, 11.00-17.30 Sat*.

Puppet Theatre Barge
Bookings and details from 78 Middleton Rd E8. 071-249 6876. A marionette theatre in a converted Thames barge, which has regular moorings at Little Venice *Sep-May*. From *May-Sep* the barge is moored at different places on the waterways and its position is listed in the London entertainment guides. Performances *Sat & Sun during term time and Mon-Sun during school hols*.

Puppet Theatre, Battersea Arts Centre (BAC)
Lavender Hill SW11. 071-228 5335. Information and advice resource centre *open 14.00-18.00 Mon-Fri*. Collection of puppets on permanent display. Book and video library on puppetry. Children's drama class 'Acting Around' *10.30-12.30 Sat* for 9-14 year olds (book in advance). Live theatre performance *14.30 Sat*.

Riverside Studios
Crisp Rd W6. 081-748 3354. An exciting programme of children's plays, puppets, music, story-telling and dancing on *Sat*. Special events for children throughout the year.

Royal National Theatre   5 A4
South Bank SE1. 071-928 2252. Normally at least one production for children or family audiences in the repertoire at any one time. Education packs available for every production. Also workshops.

Tricycle Theatre
269 Kilburn High Rd NW6. 071-328 1000. Fun children's shows every *Sat 11.30 & 14.00,* plus two productions per year by the Tricycle themselves, put on at *half terms. Children under 7 yrs must be accompanied by a paying adult*. Term time and half term workshops. Essential to book in advance. Wheelchair access and an induction loop for deaf children.

Unicorn Theatre for Children 0207 607 8753
4 F3
Arts Theatre, Great Newport St WC2. 071-836 3334. Well-established children's theatre which presents plays (often specially written for the Unicorn Theatre) and other entertainment for 4-12 year-olds. Public performances *11.00 & 14.30 Sat and 14.30 Sun* (extra performances during *school holidays*). Performances for schools at *13.30 Tue, Wed, Thur and 10.15 Wed & Fri*. Also a children's club which organises workshop sessions.

Watermans Arts Centre
40 High St, Brentford, Middx. 081-568 1176. *Saturday afternoon* theatre. Pantomime season *every Dec.*

Young Vic Theatre 5 B5
66 The Cut SE1. 071-928 6363. Repertory company putting on a good choice of re-interpreted classics, new experimental theatre, contemporary European work, alternative Christmas family shows, and work by visiting companies. Has a comprehensive programme of debates, workshops, dance and exhibitions and has strong educational links.

★ *Films* ★ ★ ★ ★ ★ ★ ★ ★ ★ ★ ★ ★ ★ ★

Remember there are age limits for certain films: U = suitable for all ages; PG = parental guidance advised and unsuitable for young children; 12 = suitable for 12 years and over; 15 = suitable for 15 years and over; 18 = suitable for 18 years and over.
Saturday morning cinema clubs show children's films at cheap prices and many West End cinemas have half-price tickets on *Mon,* and cheaper tickets for performances *before 18.00.*

Always check details before setting off. See *Time Out* and *What's On* to find out what films are showing and their times. The following show a range of films from old black and white classics, sci-fi movies and comedies to animation.

Barbican 5 D1

Silk St EC2. 071-638 4141. Children's cinema club on *Sat;* films for members *14.30*.

Clapham Picture House

Venn St SW4. 071-498 2242. Children's matinées *Sat lunchtimes*.

National Film Theatre 5 A4

South Bank SE1. 071-928 3232. Junior matinées normally *Sat & Sun afternoons*.

Rio Cinema Dalston

107 Kingland High St E8. 071-254 6677. Children's film club on *Sat mornings*. Club stewards look after unaccompanied children.

Riverside Studios

Crisp Rd W6. 081-748 3354. *Sat afternoon 14.00* is children's cinema slot. A more unusual selection of films here including foreign films.

SPECIALIST FILMS

Check the following for details, as most have showings on an irregular basis.

British Museum 4 F1

Great Russell St WC1. 071-636 1555. Mostly films on exhibitions, permanent and temporary.

Imperial War Museum 5 B6

Lambeth Rd SE1. 071-416 5000. Shows films on *Sat & Sun*.

Museum of Mankind 4 D3

6 Burlington Gdns W1. 071-323 8043. Films about people from all over the world.

Natural History Museum 6 D1

Exhibition Rd SW7. 071-938 9123. Good series of geographical films throughout the year on *Tue, Thur & Sat*. Phone for details.

★ *Concerts* ★ ★ ★ ★ ★ ★ ★ ★ ★ ★ ★ ★ ★

Several organisations arrange children's concerts, mainly classical though. But also look out for steel bands, brass bands and jazz bands at *summer* festivals in the parks. For details of pop concerts look in *Melody Maker, New Musical Express* and *Time Out*. Jazz events are listed by Jazz Services, 5 Dryden St WC2 (071-829 8352/3/4). This organisation is a central source of information for jazz music promoters and jazz fans. Some churches have regular *lunchtime* concerts and these are usually free. To check times phone the City of London Information Centre, St Paul's Churchyard EC4 (071-606 3030).

Youth and Music is an organisation worth knowing about. On their membership scheme they offer seats for 13 year-olds upwards at special discount prices. Most of the tickets are for classical, jazz or folk music plus West End musicals, dance and theatre. They can be contacted at 28 Charing Cross Rd WC2 (071-379 6722).

Arthur Davison Orchestral Concerts
Fairfield Hall, Croydon, Surrey. 081-688 9291. Orchestral concerts for children – a selection of short pieces using a wide variety of instruments. A good way of introducing children to music. Season tickets available for seven concerts which take place at *11.00 Sat.*

Ernest Read Concerts for Children   5 A4
Ernest Read Music Association, 9 Cotsford Ave, New Malden, Surrey KT3 5EU. 081-942 0318. Orchestral concerts for children over 7 held at the Royal Festival Hall. A varied range of music including theme concerts, stories put to music and choirs. Season tickets available for concerts, *Oct-May,* but tickets are issued from *May.* Advisable to book in advance as concerts are very popular: 081-336 0777.

Morley College Family Concerts   5 B6
61 Westminster Bridge Rd SE1. 071-928 8501. Series of informal concerts designed to introduce children and parents to a wide variety of music and dance, from classical to pop, ethnic to electronic. Season tickets available for eight monthly concerts, *Oct-Apr 10.30-12.30 Sat.* Tickets issued in *Sep,* also at the door.

Music for Youth
4 Blade Mews, Deodar Road SW15. 081-870 9624. Every *Nov* over 1200 talented young performers chosen from the National Festival of Music for Youth on the South Bank appear in three public concerts at the Royal Albert Hall.

Piccolo Concert Club
28 The Grove, Teddington, Middx. 081-943 1577. This is a club for 7-12 year-olds. Professional musicians give recitals and talks in a very friendly and informal atmosphere, so the concerts are both interesting and fun, as well as being brilliant musically.

★ *Radio & TV Shows* ★ ★ ★ ★ ★ ★ ★ ★ ★

If you want to join the crowd on *Going Live* or *Top of the Pops* or watch your favourite radio programme going on air, write enclosing an sae and preference of programme to one of the following:

BBC Radio & Television   1 D6
Ticket Unit, Broadcasting House, Portland Place W1.

Capital Radio   1 E5
Euston Tower, Euston Rd NW1.

Carlton Television
071-615 1515. Programmes are made by various production companies, but they will refer you to the relevant contact for tickets.

London Weekend Television   5 B4
Kent House, Upper Ground SE1. 071-620 1620.

★ *Dance* ★ ★ ★ ★ ★ ★ ★ ★ ★ ★ ★ ★ ★ ★ ★

London has a world-wide reputation for ballet and modern dance; below are some of the main venues.

London Coliseum   4 F3
St Martin's Lane WC2. 071-836 3161. Home of the London Festival Ballet season every year as well as the Nureyev Festival. Also puts on ballet productions by foreign dance companies.

The Place   1 F4
17 Duke's Rd WC1. 071-387 0161. Box office: 071-387 0031. The home base of the London Contemporary Dance Theatre. Known for its experimental and foreign productions.

Royal Opera House, Covent Garden   4 F2
Bow St WC2. 071-240 1066. The Royal Ballet Company performs here. You can see the great names in ballet in suitably lush surroundings.

Sadler's Wells Theatre   2 C4
Rosebery Ave EC1. 071-278 8916. Base of the London City Ballet; also has visiting companies such as the Ballet Rambert.

★ *Discos* ★ ★ ★ ★ ★ ★ ★ ★ ★ ★ ★ ★ ★ ★

Jo Smo's
29 Chiswick High Rd W4. 081-747 3934. Dance and music club 'n BeTwEEN' for 12-17 year olds. *Open 18.30-22.30 Wed. Closed certain times of the year so phone for details.*

Roller Disco
Roehampton Recreation Centre, Laverstoke Gdns SW15. 081-871 7672. Roller disco with competitions, prizes and games. Last *Sat* of the month *18.30-20.00* for families and under 12s, *20.00-21.30* for over 12s and faster skaters. Take your own skates.

★ *Circuses* ★ ★ ★ ★ ★ ★ ★ ★ ★ ★ ★ ★ ★

There are no permanent circuses in London; the nearest is at Chessington World of Adventures (see *Fun Days Out* on page

77). However, circuses are frequently held in London's parks and open spaces.

CIRCUS WORKSHOPS

Master the art of juggling, unicycling and tightrope walking. The following offer classes throughout the year plus *summer* workshops.

Circus Space
39-41 North Rd N7. 071-700 0868. Classes in tumbling, flying trapeze and acrobatic balance for age 6 upwards.

Jackson's Lane Circus Skills Workshops
Jackson's Lane Community Centre, 269a Archway Rd N6. 081-340 5226. A variety of workshops including tightrope walking, unicycling, juggling and stiltwalking for age 5 upwards.

Albert and Friends Instant Circus
36 Windermere Court, Lonsdale Rd SW13. 081-741 5471. Circus skills for age 3 upwards.

★ *Street Entertainment* ★ ★ ★ ★ ★ ★ ★

There's plenty of free entertainment around Covent Garden WC2 (**4 F3**). Jugglers, musicians, fire-eaters, trick cyclists and other buskers perform throughout the day. Punch and Judy shows on *Sat & Sun*.

★Activities & Interests

★ *American Football* ★ ★ ★ ★ ★ ★ ★ ★ ★

Junior American Football Association
c/o Duncan Hill, 7 Woodhouse Lane, Broomfield,
Chelmsford, Essex. For 10-18 year-olds. Please send an sae.

★ *Archaeology & History* ★ ★ ★ ★ ★ ★ ★

If you want to natter with your neighbour about Neolithic
monuments or reminisce about Roman ruins, then archaeology is for you.
The best way to get experience and maybe take part in a dig
is to join the junior section of an archaeological society – for
local clubs enquire at your nearest library or contact the
organisations below:
Council for British Archaeology
Bowes Morrell House, 111 Walmgate, York. (0904) 671417.
Publishes *British Archaeological News,* a newsletter and
calendar of excavations. However, most digs advertised
here are only really for 16 plus. Also has a guide to university
courses in the subject – please send an sae.
Heritage Explorer   **4 B2**
English Heritage, Keysign House, 429 Oxford Street W1.

071-973 3000. Junior part of the English Heritage membership scheme. Special section in their magazine devoted to Heritage Explorer members. As with senior members you can visit the English Heritage properties free.

London & Middlesex Archaeological   **5 D1**
Society (LAMAS)
Young LAMAS, c/o MOLAS, Number One London Wall EC2. 081-505 1241. A lively society. The junior section for 9-16 year-olds organises workshops, activities and visits on *Saturdays and during school holidays* and you'll receive a regular newsletter.

Young Archaeologists' Club
Bowes Morrell House, 111 Walmgate, York. (0904) 671417. For 9-16 year-olds. The club, linked with British Archaeology, organises visits to sites, fieldwork and lectures (usually outside London). Magazine with news from all around the world.

London Wall Walk   **5 D1**
EC2. The best place to see the remains of the Roman and medieval city walls. You can buy a guide from the Museum of London shop before you head off and there are information panels along the walk. The route takes about *1½ hours* to complete. Phone 071-600 3699 for details.

★ *Archery* ★ ★ ★ ★ ★ ★ ★ ★ ★ ★ ★ ★ ★

Grand National Archery Society
National Agricultural Centre, Stoneleigh, Kenilworth, Warks. (0203) 696631. Junior sections within the club will send details of clubs and events near you.

★ *Arts & Crafts* ★ ★ ★ ★ ★ ★ ★ ★ ★ ★ ★

You can do all sorts of arts and crafts in London. If brass rubbing or puppets are of particular interest, they are under separate headings in this chapter. See also *Community Centres* on page 94.

Battersea Community Arts Centre (BAC)
Old Town Hall, Lavender Hill SW11. 071-223 6557. Arts and crafts workshops *every Sat.*

Bethnal Green Museum of Childhood
Cambridge Heath Rd E2. 081-980 2415. Open house workshop in the art room *every Sat.* Workshop leaders suggest activities to children aged 3+. *Open 10.00-17.50, 14.30-17.50 Sun.*

Camden Arts Centre
Arkwright Rd NW3. 071-435 2643. *Sat morning and after-*

noon sessions for 5-16 year-olds in painting and drawing, sculpture and ceramics. *After-school* classes plus courses during *school hols*. Local schools visit during term time.

Chelsea Pottery   **6 F3**
13 Radnor Walk SW3. 071-352 1366. Good, well-established studio. Children's classes on *Sat 10.00-13.00 & 14.00-17.00*. Minimum age 5. Membership.

Susan Meyer-Michael
99 North End Rd NW11. 081-455 0817. Pottery and clay modelling. Small groups or individual lessons. Sessions by arrangement only.

★ *Astronomy* ★ ★ ★ ★ ★ ★ ★ ★ ★ ★ ★ ★

If you are interested in space travel and what lies beyond the earth then astronomy is for you. Greenwich Planetarium (Old Royal Observatory) and the London Planetarium show projections of the sky and stars, and there is an annual Astronomy Exhibition held in London each *Feb* (see *Calendar* on page 16).

British Astronomical Association   **4 D3**
Burlington House, Piccadilly W1. 071-734 4145. Members are aged 7-90. Monthly meetings from *Oct-Jun* as well as *weekend courses*. Newsletter *six times a year*.

Hampstead Scientific Society
Treasurer, 22 Flask Walk NW3. 071-794 9341. Organises talks and outings and also has its own observatory at Lower Terrace NW3. Junior membership. Monthly meetings at Burgh House *Sep-Jun*. Observatory *open Sep-Apr 20.00-22.00 Fri & Sat, 11.00-13.00 Sun, weather permitting*. Phone the Observatory on 081-346 1056 for details.

Junior Astronomical Society
36 Fairway, Keyworth, Notts. Open to interested beginners of any age. Meets *four times a year* in London. Quarterly magazine and bi-monthly newsletter sent to members. Annual subscription. Write to the Secretary at the above address for details.

★ *Athletics* ★ ★ ★ ★ ★ ★ ★ ★ ★ ★ ★ ★ ★

Amateur Athletics Association
225A Bristol Road, Edgbaston, Birmingham, West Midlands. 021-440 5000. There are almost 2000 clubs and meetings throughout the country and the association will be able to recommend one near you. Or you can talk to someone at your nearest sports centre. For 7 year-olds upwards.

Watching
Major international events are held at:
Crystal Palace Sports Centre, Ledrington Rd SE19. 081-778
0131. The Athletics Association will give you details of club
meetings and a diary of events.

★ *Badminton* ★ ★ ★ ★ ★ ★ ★ ★ ★ ★ ★ ★

English Schools Badminton Association
National Badminton Centre, Bradwell Rd, Loughton Lodge,
Milton Keynes, Bucks. (0908) 568822. Will give you information about any tournaments or clubs in your district. If your
school is not a member of the above, contact the
Badminton Association of England at the same address and
number.

★ *Baseball & Softball* ★ ★ ★ ★ ★ ★ ★ ★ ★ ★

British Baseball Federation
(0482) 643 551. Details of clubs throughout the UK such as
the Golders Green Sox and the Barnes Stormers.

★ *Basketball* ★ ★ ★ ★ ★ ★ ★ ★ ★ ★ ★ ★

English Basketball Association
48 Bradford Road, Stanninley, Leeds LS28 6DF. (0532)
361166. Will give you names of clubs if your school doesn't
belong to the English Schools Basketball Association.
Also check out the various sports centres on page 109 as
many of them have basketball facilities.

★ *Boating* ★ ★ ★ ★ ★ ★ ★ ★ ★ ★ ★ ★ ★ ★

If you feel like a relaxing afternoon there are quite a few metropolitan centres where anyone can hire a boat, pedalo or canoe:

Crystal Palace Park SE19 (in *summer*)
Finsbury Park Lake N4
Regent's Park Lake NW1   **1 B4**
Serpentine Boating Lake, Hyde Park W2   **3 F4**
Westminster Boating Base, Dinorvic Wharf,   **7 D4**
136 Grosvenor Rd SW1. 071-821 7389. Youth programme for 10-23 year-olds including canoeing and sailing.

★ *Book Clubs* ★ ★ ★ ★ ★ ★ ★ ★ ★ ★ ★ ★

Bookworm
W Heffer & Sons, 20 Trinity St, Cambridge. (0223) 358351. Bookworm is for 7-12 year-olds. Early Worm for 0-7 year-olds. Both clubs are run through schools or groups.
Puffin School Book Club   **3 C6**
c/o Penguin Books Ltd, 27 Wright's Lane W8. 071-938 2200. Well-established book club for children up to age 13. Encourages an interest in reading and books. There are three clubs, all run through schools: Fledgeling (0-6 years), Flight (7-9 years) and Post (9-13 years).
Scholastic Publications Ltd
Westfield Road, Southam, Leamington Spa, Warks. (092681) 3910. Promotes a variety of book clubs: Seesaw (0-6 yrs), Lucky (7-9 yrs), Hip (9-12 yrs) and Scene (12+ yrs). Monthly *Club News*. You can join through your school.

★ *Boxing* ★ ★ ★ ★ ★ ★ ★ ★ ★ ★ ★ ★ ★ ★

London Boxing Association
56 Comber Grove SE5. 071-252 7008. The association will put you in touch with local clubs. Minimum age 11.
Watching
Important fights are staged at Wembley, Earl's Court and the Royal Albert Hall. The newspaper *Boxing News* lists bouts.

★ *Brass Rubbing* ★ ★ ★ ★ ★ ★ ★ ★ ★ ★ ★

You can learn how to make your own rubbings at brass rubbing centres, which provide replicas of many historic monumental brasses plus everything you need. The cost of rubbings is graded according to the size of the brasses. Once experienced, search out brasses in old churches all over the country, but ask for permission first.

All Hallows-by-the-Tower   **5 F3**
Byward St EC3. 071-481 2928. At the west end of the church is an appealing assembly of about 30 brasses, although space allows for no more than 10 people to make rubbings at any one time. Free instruction available. *Book for groups. Open 11.00-16.30 Mon-Sat, 12.30-17.00 Sun.* Charge.

London Brass Rubbing Centre   **4 F3**
St Martin-in-the-Fields WC2. 071-437 6023. Replicas on display of 70 British and European brasses ranging from animal figures, children and wool merchants to a crusader knight which stands 2.1 metres (7ft) tall. Instruction available. *Open 10.00-18.00 Mon-Sat, 12.00-18.00 Sun.* Charge.

★ *Canoeing* ★ ★ ★ ★ ★ ★ ★ ★ ★ ★ ★ ★ ★

British Canoe Union
Adbolton Lane, West Bridgeford, Nottingham, Notts. (0602) 821100. They will send you a list of canoeing centres in the UK. There are clubs that families and individuals can join.

★ *Chess* ★ ★ ★ ★ ★ ★ ★ ★ ★ ★ ★ ★ ★ ★

4 Nations Chess League
PO Box 175, Croydon. 081-688 3119. For information regarding chess nationwide.

★ *Climbing* ★ ★ ★ ★ ★ ★ ★ ★ ★ ★ ★ ★ ★

British Mountaineering Council
Crawford House, Precinct Centre, Booth Street East, Manchester. 061-273 5835. Details of introductory courses in mountaineering and rock climbing for 12-16 year-olds *during the summer hols.* Family membership scheme.

Brixton Recreation Centre
Brixton Station Rd SW9. 071-926 9780. One inside wall for climbing without ropes. Coaching available on *Wed evenings.* Minimum age 7 yrs.

Michael Sobell Sports Centre
Hornsey Rd N7. 071-609 2166. One wall with climbing and abseiling to all standards. *Phone for details of session times.*

North London Rescue Commando Centre
Cordova Road E3. 081-980 0289. A large number and variety

of walls from beginner to competition standard. Age restrictions apply – *essential to phone for details*.

★ *Community Centres* ★ ★ ★ ★ ★ ★ ★ ★

These are centres which organise a great variety of activities for both children and adults; somewhere you can go to join a club, learn a new skill or simply use the facilities.

Battersea Arts Centre (BAC)
Old Town Hall, Lavender Hill SW11. 071-223 6557. *Sat* is children's day with workshops, acting classes and puppetry plus shows and films. Also workshops during *school hols*.

Inter-Action Social Enterprise Trust   5 B3
HMS President (1918), nr Blackfriars Bridge, Victoria Embankment EC4. 071-583 2652. Facilities for computing, children's workshops and a hands-on technology centre.

Jackson's Lane Community Centre
269a Archway Rd N6. 081-340 5226. *After school and holiday* workshops for children including dance, arts and crafts, plus an excellent programme of visiting theatre and dance groups. Children's theatre *Sat mornings*. Also run a parent and toddlers group.

Riverside Studios
Crisp Rd W6. 081-748 3354. Spacious arts centre which organises children's educational visits and holiday activities. Children's entertainment at *weekends*.

★ *Cricket* ★ ★ ★ ★ ★ ★ ★ ★ ★ ★ ★ ★ ★ ★

English Schools Cricket Association
c/o Mr Lake, 38 Mill House, Woods Lane, Cottingham, North Humberside. (0482) 844446. The governing body for cricket in schools.

MCC Indoor Cricket School
Lord's Cricket Ground, St John's Wood Rd NW8. 071-286 3649. Coaching for all ages from 8 years upwards, beginners and advanced.

Remember many of London's parks have practice nets which can be booked through the park authorities.
Watching
During *summer*, international and county matches are played at:
Lord's Cricket Ground, St John's Wood Rd NW8. 071-289 1615.
Oval Cricket Ground, Kennington Oval SE11. 071-582 6660.
For tours of Lord's Cricket Ground and the cricket memorial gallery see *Behind the Scenes* on page 63.

★ *Croquet* ★ ★ ★ ★ ★ ★ ★ ★ ★ ★ ★ ★ ★ ★

The Croquet Association
Hurlingham Club, Ranelagh Gardens SW6. 071-736 3148. A game which is more fun than it looks! They will send you a complete list of local clubs and how to get involved with them.

★ *Cross-country Skiing* ★ ★ ★ ★ ★ ★ ★ ★

London Nordic Ski Club
8 Pebble Drive, Millbrook Village, Didcot, Oxon. (0235) 818833. Organise sessions which are usually held in Battersea Park to learn necessary techniques. They train using roller skis. Phone for details. Minimum age 5.

★ *Cycling* ★ ★ ★ ★ ★ ★ ★ ★ ★ ★ ★ ★ ★ ★

Bicycle Moto-cross (BMX)
The BMX Association, National Office, 61 Mayfield Gdns, Hanwell W7. 081-813 2838. Can provide information on London clubs and tracks for BMX fans. They also organise competitions and publish the magazine *Extra BMX*.

British Cycling Federation
36 Rockingham Rd, Kettering, Northants. (0536) 412211. A society for all sorts of cyclists: racers, commuters, tourists and general leisure riders. They offer members comprehensive insurance, an annual handbook with advice and tips, a coaching service and information on racing.

Cycling Proficiency Tests
Most boroughs organise their own cycling proficiency lessons and tests for 9-13 year-olds. Certificates are issued to those who pass tests in the theory and practice of safe bicycling. Enquire at your local town hall for details or contact the Royal Society for the Prevention of Accidents (ROSPA), Cannon House, The Priory Queensway, Birmingham, West Midlands, for details of their schemes. 021-200 2461.

Eastway Cycle Circuit
Temple Mills Lane E15. 081-534 6085. Coaching to improve cycling ability and a training ground for more experienced racing cyclists. Book through schools. Bikes, including mountain bikes, for hire and BMX race track. Minimum age 9. *Open Mar-Oct 08.00-20.00 Mon-Sun; Nov-Feb 08.00-16.00 Mon-Sun.*

Hiring Bikes
If you're under 18 and want to hire a bike, you'll need to be a competent rider and put down a large deposit. You might

need a guarantee from your parents as well. Phone **Kidsline** on 071-222 8070 for hire shops near you.

★ *Dancing* ★ ★ ★ ★ ★ ★ ★ ★ ★ ★ ★ ★ ★ ★

Dance Works   4 B2
16 Balderton St W1. 071-629 6183. *Sat* classes for 5-10 year-olds in classical ballet. *Mon evening* classes in tap and jazz for 3-5 yrs, 5-9 yrs, 9-16 yrs. *Thur evening* classes in contemporary dance for 5-10 yrs.

Imperial Society of Teachers of Dancing   2 A4
Euston Hall, Birkenhead St WC1. 071-837 9967. Teachers of ballet by the Cecchetti method and other types of dance. Send an sae for a list of teachers and local dance schools.

Islington Dance Factory
2 Parkhurst Rd N7. 071-607 0561. Multi-arts centre with classes for adults and children. Ballet for children over 6, contemporary for 12+.

The Place   1 F4
17 Duke's Rd WC1. 071-388 8956. The Young Place offers classes in creative dance and composition, contemporary, jazz and classical ballet for ages 5-8, 8-10, 10-12 and 13-18 on *Sat mornings*. Also the home of the London Contemporary Dance Theatre. A new Youth Dance Group offers extensive and exciting dance experience for 10-16 year-olds.

Royal Academy of Dancing   6 D6
36 Battersea Square SW11. 071-223 0091. Classes in classical ballet for 5-17 year-olds, leading to RAD grade examinations. Entry to all classes is by audition only. Send an sae for lists of teachers, addressed to the Registration & Membership Department (above address).

Royal Ballet School
White Lodge, Richmond Park, Surrey. 081-748 6335. This is the Lower School for 11-16 year-olds. Auditions are held to determine potential for classical ballet training. If you are accepted you will receive a full-time general education in addition to being taught classical ballet. Telephone for a prospectus.

★ *Drama* ★ ★ ★ ★ ★ ★ ★ ★ ★ ★ ★ ★ ★ ★

Anna Scher Children's Theatre   2 C2
70-72 Barnsbury Rd N1. 071-278 2101. *After school* classes for children from age 6 upwards in improvisation, poetry,

production, stage technique and the theory of the theatre. The lessons are imaginatively and thoroughly planned. There is a long waiting list for places.

Arts Junior School
West London Institute of Higher Education, 300 St Margaret's Rd, Twickenham, Middx. 081-891 0121. Drama class on *Sat mornings* for age 9 upwards – covers acting, stage management and lighting.

Greenwich and Lewisham Young People's Theatre
Burrage Rd SE18. 081-854 1316. Lively *evening* workshops *Mon-Thur during term time* for 11-15s, 15-20s and 18-25s. Drama and visual arts. Occasional performances by outside groups.

Group 64 Youth Theatre
203b Upper Richmond Rd SW15. 081-788 6943. Theatre in a converted church. Play writing, improvisation and drama games for 9-15 year-olds *Sat mornings*. Classes for children aged 15+ held *19.30 Wed during term time.*

Mountview Theatre School
Ralph Richardson Memorial Studios, Clarendon Road, Wood Green N22. 081-889 8110. *Sat morning* activities for ages 6-8 and 9-12. *Sat afternoon* stage dance for 7+. *Easter* and *summer* children's workshops.

National Youth Theatre
Holloway Rd N7. 071-281 3863. For 14-21 year-olds interested in any aspect of the theatre. Auditions are held in *Feb & Mar* to select the casts of plays to be rehearsed and performed during the *summer hols*. Closing date for applications *Dec.*

Polka Children's Theatre
240 The Broadway SW19. 081-543 4888. Workshops and courses for 3 year-olds upwards. Music, clowning and puppet-making may be on the agenda.

Questors Theatre
Mattock Lane W5. 081-567 0011. Excellent amateur theatre club with drama playgroups on *Sat mornings* for 5-9 year-olds. Emphasis on imaginative play and role-playing activities. Junior Drama Workshops are held on *weekday evenings* and *Sun mornings*. Role-playing, improvisation and acting exercises. Groups graded according to age and experience.

Theatre Royal Stratford East
Gerry Raffles Sq E15. 081-534 0310. Theatre workshop for 9-14 year-olds on *Sat mornings* and on *Mon evenings* for those aged 14 upwards. Drama, games, mime, scriptwork, maskwork. Usually lead to performances in the theatre.

Unicorn Theatre for Children   4 E3
6-7 Great Newport St WC2. 071-379 3280. Improvisation and craft workshops for children from 4-12 years. Also stages plays for children aged 4-12.

Upstream Children's Theatre
Ilderton School, Varcoe Rd, off Old Kent Rd SE16 (entrance in Ilderton Rd). 071-232 2869. Educational drama and theatre workshops for 3-12 year-olds. Workshops include improvisation, story-telling, stage make-up, puppetry, music.

Watermans Arts Centre
40 High St, Brentford, Middx. 081-568 1176. Theatre Club – drama, theatre games, improvisation. Split into age groups – *Sat mornings* for 9-15 year-olds upwards, *Sat afternoons* for 5-8 year-olds. Children's video workshop *Sat morning* for 9-13 year-olds. Also visual arts workshops *during school hols* covering areas as diverse as mask making and story-telling.

★ *Fencing* ★ ★ ★ ★ ★ ★ ★ ★ ★ ★ ★ ★ ★ ★

Amateur Fencing Association
1 Baron's Gate, 33 Rothschild Rd W4. 081-742 3032. Provides a list of local clubs and a fixture list. The Schools Fencing Union can be reached here too.

★ *Film and video-making* ★ ★ ★ ★ ★ ★ ★

Children's Film Unit
9 Hamilton House, 66 Upper Richmond Rd SW15. 081-871 2006. Organises movie making for 8-16 year-olds, involving

acting, camera skills, sound, make-up, continuity, script-writing and all the other activities that go into making a film. There are workshop sessions every *Sat* and an annual full-length movie made in the *summer holidays*.

Star Trax 4 E3

The Trocadero, 13 Coventry St W1. 071-287 0854. You, your children and friends can become stars in your own pop video. Choose from over 150 songs – and then dance, perform or mime to Whitney Houston or the Beatles. Quite expensive but good value and you can have great fun rehearsing, then in the studio – and of course watching the video at home! *Open 11.00-23.30 Mon-Sun.*

★ *Fishing* ★ ★ ★ ★ ★ ★ ★ ★ ★ ★ ★ ★ ★ ★

If you are over 12, you will need to have a Thames Water Board licence to fish in most waters in London. You can get one cheaply in most fishing tackle shops which will allow you to try your luck in the Thames and the canals. You'll need a different licence to fish in the royal parks, though some are free. Park attendants can advise you.

For further information contact:

London Anglers' Association

Forest Road Hall, Hervey Park Rd E17. 081-520 7477. Membership entitles you to fish on the LAA's 100 miles of water, pits and lakes. For full details contact the association.

National Federation of Anglers

Halliday House, Egginton Junction, Derbyshire DE65 6GU. (0283) 734735. The NFA is the governing body for coarse fishing and will put you in touch with relevant organisations.

Thames Water Authority

PO Box 436 Swindon, Wilts. (0734) 593333.

Walthamstow Reservoir

Ferry Lane N17. 081-808 1527. Six different waters for coarse fishing, three for trout. Permits for a whole day or whole season for coarse; whole or half day for trout (not season). No children under 8; under 16s should be accompanied by an adult, but this is at the discretion of the management. *Open 07.30-½ hr after sunset.*

★ *Flying* ★ ★ ★ ★ ★ ★ ★ ★ ★ ★ ★ ★ ★ ★

London School of Flying
Elstree Aerodrome, Elstree, Herts. 081-953 4343. You can start at any age, but you have to be 17 before you can go solo. Has two affiliated clubs at Biggin Hill and one at Denham, Blackbush, Redhill and Cranfield. Membership of one entitles you to use of all seven. *Phone to find out more about lessons.*

★ *Folk Music & Dancing* ★ ★ ★ ★ ★ ★ ★

English Folk Song & Dance Society   1 C2
Cecil Sharp House, 2 Regent's Park Rd NW1. 071-485 2206. The Hobby Horse Club is the children's section. Members receive a badge, a birthday card, newsletters and a list of festivals where there will be children's events. There is a children's day of dance held *once a month.*

★ *Football* ★ ★ ★ ★ ★ ★ ★ ★ ★ ★ ★ ★ ★

Football Association   3 D3
16 Lancaster Gate W2. 071-262 4542. Each county has a youth section that the Football Association will put you in touch with or you can contact the English Schools Association, 4a Eastgate St, Stafford, Staffs. (0785) 51142. Almost all sports centres (see page 109) offer five-a-side football as one of their activities.
Watching
London offers some of the best football in the world, with usually three or four first division clubs to follow. Here are some of the main London clubs:
Arsenal Football Club, Avenell Rd, Highbury N5. 071-226 0304.
Charlton Football Club, The Valley, Floyd Road, Charlton SE7. 081-293 4567.
Chelsea Football Club, Stamford Bridge SW6. 071-385 5545.
Crystal Palace, Selhurst Park, Whitehorse Lane SE25. 081-653 4462.
Fulham Football Club, Craven Cottage, Stevenage Rd SW6. 071-736 6561.
Millwall Football Club, The Den, Zampa Rd SE16. 071-232 1222.
Queen's Park Rangers Football Club, South Africa Rd W12. 081-743 0262.
Tottenham Hotspur Football Club, 748 High Rd N17. 081-365 5000.
West Ham United Football Club, Boleyn Ground, Green St E13. 081-472 2740.

Wimbledon Football Club, Selhurst Park, Whitehorse Lane SE25. 081-771 2233.

If you contact the managers of these clubs, you may be allowed to watch practice games.

For guided tours of Wembley Stadium see *Behind the Scenes* on page 63.

★ *Games centres* ★ ★ ★ ★ ★ ★ ★ ★ ★ ★

Alien War   4 E3
The Trocadero, 13 Coventry St W1. 071-437 2678. Role play theatre in which you are led through an 'alien' world by your 'trained and armed space marine'. Await the unexpected. *Open 10.30-24.00 Mon-Sun. No admittance for children under 8; children under 12 must be accompanied by an adult.*

Funland   4 E3
The Trocadero, 13 Coventry St W1. 071-287 8913. Europe's largest, most hi-tech games centre full of fun and thrills for all the family. Old favourites like dodgems and kiddy rides alongside video games, virtuality simulator rides and electromechanical games.

Quasar at the Trocadero   4 E3
The Trocadero, 13 Coventry St W1. 071-734 8151. Hide and seek with laser guns. A live action game in which players are equipped with a specially designed "Quasar-gun" and back and chest packs. Points are scored by de-activating the opposing team within a space fantasy arena. Each game lasts $\frac{1}{2}$-hour. *Open 10.00-24.00 Mon-Thur & Sun, 10.00-01.00 Fri & Sat.* Not suitable for under 7s.

★ *Go-karting* ★ ★ ★ ★ ★ ★ ★ ★ ★ ★ ★

British Motor Sports Council
Motor Sports House, Riverside Park, Colnbrook, Slough. (0753) 681736. Go-karting for children from 8 years upwards. Supply information on fixture lists and regulations, as well as details about safety.

★ *Gymnastics* ★ ★ ★ ★ ★ ★ ★ ★ ★ ★ ★

Most sports centres (see page 109) provide classes and coaching for all ages, including under 5s.

Amateur Gymnastics Association
Write to: Mrs J Thatch, Secretary, 4 Victoria Rd, Chingford E4. 081-529 1142. Organising body for the sport which should provide advice and a list of clubs.

★ *Hockey* ★ ★ ★ ★ ★ ★ ★ ★ ★ ★ ★ ★ ★ ★ ★

Hockey Association
Norfolk House, 102 Saxon Gate West, Milton Keynes MK9
2EP. (0908) 241 100. For a list of clubs.

★ *Ice Hockey* ★ ★ ★ ★ ★ ★ ★ ★ ★ ★ ★ ★ ★

British Ice Hockey Association
517 Christchurch Rd, Bournemouth, Dorset. (0202) 395946.
Contact them for names of clubs with a junior section for
the under 16s.

★ *Ice Skating* ★ ★ ★ ★ ★ ★ ★ ★ ★ ★ ★ ★ ★

Broadgate Ice   **5 F1**
Eldon St EC2. 071-588 6565. London's only open-air ice rink.
There's loads of refreshment spots all round the rink when
you've had enough of tearing around. Individual and group
lessons can be arranged. The exciting Canadian game of
Broomball, a gentler version of ice hockey, is played here.
*Open mid Nov-Mar 12.00-15.00 Mon; 12.00-15.00 & 16.00-
19.30 Tue-Fri; 11.00-13.00, 14.00-16.00 & 17.00-19.00 Sat &
Sun. Closed Apr-mid Nov.*
Michael Sobell Ice Rink
Hornsey Rd N7. 071-609 2166. Small but relatively inexpen-
sive rink; special school sessions *Wed & Fri 16.00-17.30.
Opening hours vary, phone for details.*
National Skating Association   **2 E5**
15-27 Gee St EC1. 071-253 3824. The governing body of the
sport which provides information and advice.
The following centres have ice rinks. You can usually hire
boots on the door. They will take skaters from 3 years
upwards.
Queens Ice Skating Club   **3 C3**
Queensway W2. 071-229 0172. *Open 10.00-16.30 & 19.30-
22.00 Mon-Fri; 10.00-17.00 & 19.30-22.30 Sat & Sun. Closes
22.00 Sun.*
Streatham Ice Rink
386 Streatham High Rd SW16. 081-769 7771. *Open 10.00-
16.30 & 19.30-22.30 Mon-Fri; 11.00-16.45 & 20.00-23.00 Sat
& Sun.*

★ *Judo* ★ ★ ★ ★ ★ ★ ★ ★ ★ ★ ★ ★ ★ ★ ★ ★

British Judo Association
7a Rutland St, Leicester. (0533) 559669. Over 1200 clubs in
the UK.

London Judo Society
89 Lansdowne Way SW8. 071-622 0529. Contact for information on clubs nearby.

★ *Karate* ★ ★ ★ ★ ★ ★ ★ ★ ★ ★ ★ ★ ★

British Amateur Karate Association   **2 A4**
120 Cromer St WC1. 071-837 4406. Write to the above for clubs near you.

★ *Kite-flying* ★ ★ ★ ★ ★ ★ ★ ★ ★ ★ ★

The wide open spaces of Blackheath and Hampstead Heath are ideal for kite-flying. There are regular stunt kite events at Blackheath. Phone 071-275 8799 for details.

★ *Lacrosse* ★ ★ ★ ★ ★ ★ ★ ★ ★ ★ ★ ★

All England Women's Lacrosse Association
4 Western Court, Bromley Street, Digbeth, Birmingham B9 4AN. 021-773 4422. If you've never watched lacrosse, it is well worth going to an international – it's very exciting. The Lacrosse Association will give you details of local clubs and major matches.

★ *Life-saving* ★ ★ ★ ★ ★ ★ ★ ★ ★ ★ ★

Your local swimming baths should provide information about coaching and tests.
Royal Life-saving Society
Mountbatten House, Studley, Warks. (052785) 3943. They will send you information on your local branch.

★ *Martial Arts* ★ ★ ★ ★ ★ ★ ★ ★ ★ ★

Martial Arts Commission
1st Floor, Broadway House, 15-16 Deptford Broadway SE8. 081-691 3433. This is the specialist advisory body of all martial arts to the Sports Council. It has a computer data base and so can put you in touch with your local club.

★ *Music* ★ ★ ★ ★ ★ ★ ★ ★ ★ ★ ★ ★ ★

There is a professional register of music teachers which should be available in the reference section of your library.
Islington Arts Factory
2 Parkhurst Rd N7. 071-607 0561. Arts centre which

specialises in dance, music, visual art and writing. Children's music club, band workshops, kit drumming and recorder for children over 6. Lessons *after school*. Phone for details.

London College of Music

Thames Valley University, St Mary's Road, Ealing W5. 081-231 2304. *Sat morning* junior music school for children over 5. Also individual lessons for any instrument.

National Youth Jazz Orchestra   **2 A3**

Meets at the London Studio Centre, 42-50 York Way, Kings Cross on *Sat*. Two sessions – *10.30* and *14.00*. Musicians must be of a high standard. Details from 11 Victor Rd, Harrow, Middx. 081-863 2717.

National Youth Orchestra of Great Britain

Detailed information and application forms from Causeway House, Lodge Causeway, Fishponds, Bristol BS16 3HD. (0272) 650036. 11-17 year-olds can apply for an audition to be trained and once a member of the orchestra you remain so until you are 19 (subject to an annual re-audition).

Watermans Arts Centre

40 High St, Brentford, Middx. 081-568 1176. 'Pandemonium' – lively sessions which introduce under 5s to music. Phone for details.

West London Institute of Higher Education

300 St Margaret's Rd, Twickenham, Middx. 081-891 0121. Music classes: aural training, music theory, personal tuition and the opportunity to participate in the choir and instrumental ensembles. Classes on *Sat mornings* for 10-16 year-olds.

★ *Natural History & Conservation* ★ ★ ★

Many of London's parks and open spaces have animal corners, small zoos and sanctuaries (see *Out of Doors* on page 69). But if you have a particular interest, perhaps one of the organisations below can help:

Lifewatch Club   **1 C3**
London Zoo, Regent's Park NW1. 071-722 3333. For children. Membership gives free entry to London Zoo, plus the zoo magazine, special events, talks, films, discussions and outings.

London Natural History Society
Contact: Mr Barrett, Secretary, 21 Green Way, Frinton-on-Sea, Essex CO13 9AL. (0255) 674678. Covers the area within a 20-mile radius of St Paul's Cathedral. Welcomes junior members to the regular outings and meetings in London and elsewhere. Birdwatching excursions *midweek and most weekends*. Newsletter and bulletin *every two months*.

★ *Netball* ★ ★ ★ ★ ★ ★ ★ ★ ★ ★ ★ ★ ★

All England Netball Association
Netball House, 9 Paynes Park, Hitchin, Herts SG5 1EH. (0462) 442344. For the name of a club near you.

★ *Orienteering* ★ ★ ★ ★ ★ ★ ★ ★ ★ ★

A cheap and easy sport for the whole family. Events take place most *Suns*, many within London.

British Orienteering Federation
Riversdale, Dale Rd North, Darley Dale, Matlock, Derbs. (0629) 734042. Phone or write for further information.

★ *Ornithology* ★ ★ ★ ★ ★ ★ ★ ★ ★ ★ ★

Young Ornithologists' Club
c/o The Royal Society for the Protection of Birds (RSPB), The Lodge, Sandy, Beds. (0767) 680551. Junior membership (under 16) gives a badge, a bi-monthly magazine *(Bird Life)* and a chance to take part in outings to RSPB reserves and join in special projects. They also organise holiday courses. Family, school and group membership also available.

In urban areas, reservoirs have become an important habitat for birds. So get hold of a permit, dust off the binoculars and take a bus to one of Thames Water's London lakes:

Walthamstow Reservoir N17.
Walton Reservoirs, Surrey.
Phone or write to Thames Water, PO Box 436 Swindon, Wilts. (0734) 593333.

★ *Parascending* ★ ★ ★ ★ ★ ★ ★ ★ ★ ★ ★

British Association of Paragliding Clubs
The Old School Room, Loughborough Rd, Leicester. (0533) 611322. They will provide a full information pack, directory of clubs, membership application form and copy of *Skywings,* the parascending magazine.

★ *Polo* ★ ★ ★ ★ ★ ★ ★ ★ ★ ★ ★ ★ ★ ★

Equestrian Club
Church Rd, Ham Common, Richmond, Surrey. 081-940 2020. Matches are played here *every Sat morning, Sun afternoon and Thur evening from Apr-Sep.* Also regular matches on *Sun* at Ham House, see local paper for details.
Guard's Polo Club
Smith's Lawn, Windsor, Berks. (0784) 434212. You can watch the polo here from *May-Sep* on *Tue-Sun afternoons* and on *Bank hols.*

★ *Puppetry* ★ ★ ★ ★ ★ ★ ★ ★ ★ ★ ★ ★ ★

Puppet Centre Trust
Battersea Arts Centre, Old Town Hall, Lavender Hill SW11. 071-228 5335. A reference centre for everything to do with puppetry. Information and consultancy service, exhibition, library, shop and training courses for children. Bi-monthly magazine.

★ *Riding* ★ ★ ★ ★ ★ ★ ★ ★ ★ ★ ★ ★ ★ ★

Pony Club
The British Horse Society, British Equestrian Centre, Stoneleigh Park, Kenilworth, Warks. (0203) 696697. For names of riding clubs near you. Children can work towards Pony Club awards.
Alternatively, you could enjoy a ride in one of the parks. The following all have access to a London park. It is best to phone in advance as they can get booked up:
Hyde Park Riding Stables   3 E3
63 Bathurst Mews W2. 071-723 2813. Minimum age 5. You can take lessons or hire ponies here. Riding in Hyde Park.

Roehampton Riding Stables
Priory Lane SW15. 081-876 7089. Minimum age 7. Lessons on *Tue-Sun*. Riding in Richmond Park.

Ross Nye's Riding Establishment 3 E3
8 Bathurst Mews W2. 071-262 3791. Minimum age 7. Teaching stable. Riding in Hyde Park.

Trent Park Equestrian Centre
Bramley Rd, Southgate N14. 081-363 8630/9005. Minimum age 5. Riding lessons in Trent Park.

Wimbledon Village Stables
24a/b High St SW19. 081-946 8579. Minimum age 2½. Teaching stable. Classes take place on Wimbledon Common.

★ *Roller skating* ★ ★ ★ ★ ★ ★ ★ ★ ★ ★ ★ ★

Roller Disco
Roehampton Recreation Centre, Laverstoke Gdns SW15. 081-871 7672. Roller disco with competitions, prizes and games. Held on the last *Sat* of the month *18.30-20.00* for families and under 12s, *20.00-21.30* for over 12s and faster skaters. Take your own skates.

Roller Express
Unit 16, Lea Valley Trading Estate, Angel Rd, Edmonton N18. 081-807 7345. Information on session times: 081-803 1431. Huge, purpose-built roller skating rink with a burger bar, video games, shop and licensed bar for Mums and Dads. *Open 19.00-23.00 Mon, 11.30-15.30 Tue, 11.30-15.30 & 19.00-23.00 Wed, 21.00-01.00 Thur, 11.30-15.30 & 21.00-03.00 Fri, 12.30-18.00 Sat, 12.30-17.30 & 18.00-22.30 Sun.* Extra sessions during school hols. Free skate hire if required.

★ *Rounders* ★ ★ ★ ★ ★ ★ ★ ★ ★ ★ ★ ★ ★

National Rounders Association
c/o Bryan MacKinney, 3 Denehurst Avenue, Nottingham NG8 5DA. (0602) 785514. A source of information on clubs and meetings.

★ *Rowing* ★ ★ ★ ★ ★ ★ ★ ★ ★ ★ ★ ★ ★ ★

The most famous event is the Oxford v Cambridge boat race (see *Calendar* on page 17). The Head of the River event on the Thames is held in *Mar*.

Amateur Rowing Association
6 Lower Mall W6. 081-748 3632. Has details of events and clubs. However most clubs will not take junior members until they are over 10 years old.

★ *Rugby* ★ ★ ★ ★ ★ ★ ★ ★ ★ ★ ★ ★ ★ ★ ★

Rugby Football Union
Whitton Rd, Twickenham, Middx. 081-892 8161. For the name of your nearest club.
Watching
Major rugby football matches are held at the Twickenham ground (above address). The Rugby Football Union (see above) gives details of the dates.
For tours of Twickenham Rugby Football Ground see *Behind the Scenes* on page 63.

★ *Sailing* ★ ★ ★ ★ ★ ★ ★ ★ ★ ★ ★ ★ ★ ★

Royal Yachting Association
Romsey Rd, Eastleigh, Hants. (0703) 629962. Have different booklets for all kinds of sailing which list courses, clubs and sailing schools in the UK. Only really for 6 plus.

★ *Skiing* ★ ★ ★ ★ ★ ★ ★ ★ ★ ★ ★ ★ ★ ★

British Ski Slope Operator's Association
Skewbridge Ski School, Northampton Rd, Rushden, Northants. (0933) 59939.

Ski Club of Great Britain   7 B1
118 Eaton Sq SW1. 071-245 1033. They publish a list of dry-ski schools in the London area. Send an sae.
Dry ski slopes:

Alexandra Palace Ski Centre
Alexandra Park N22. 081-888 2284. One main slope with four lanes, and a smaller nursery slope. Private and group lessons available. *Open 14.00-22.00 Mon-Fri, 10.00-18.00 Sat & Sun.*

Beckton Alps
Alpine Way E6. 071-511 0351. Tuition available – there's a six-hour course for a set price. Hire of skis included in all prices but you can take your own. Really all you need is your own gloves! Bar, restaurant. *Open 10.00-22.30 Mon-Fri, 09.00-22.30 Sat & Sun.*

Crystal Palace Ski Centre
Ledrington Rd SE19. 081-778 0131. Nursery slope, courses from *Oct-Mar*. Junior ski club on *Sat* and during *school holidays*. Minimum children's boot size 3. *Open 09.00-22.00 Mon-Fri, 09.00-20.00 Sat, 09.00-18.00 Sun. Phone for details of session times.*

Hillingdon Ski Centre
Park Rd, Uxbridge, Middx. (0895) 255183. One main slope, one intermediate, two nursery and one kindergarten. Lessons can be arranged for all standards. *Open 10.00-22.00 Mon-Fri & Sun, 10.00-18.00 Sat.*

★ *Sports Centres* ★ ★ ★ ★ ★ ★ ★ ★ ★ ★

There's a huge variety of sports available in London and the best place to go is a sports centre. Each one offers dozens of different activities and they are all under cover so there is no reason for rain or cold to spoil your fun.

Look under 'Leisure Centres' in the *Yellow Pages* for the nearest place to try out a range of sporting activities. Most run special programmes in the holidays. If you want to join a more specialist society or association, contact the addresses given in this section.

Here are some of London's main sports centres:

Brixton Recreation Centre
27 Brixton Station Rd SW2. 071-926 9780. Membership not required. *Open 12.00-22.30 Mon-Fri, 09.00-20.00 Sat & Sun.*

Chelsea Sports Centre   **6 E3**
Chelsea Manor St SW3. 071-352 6985. Membership not required. *Open 07.30-22.00 Mon-Fri, 08.00-22.00 Sat, 08.00-18.30 Sun.*

Crystal Palace National Sports Centre
Ledrington Rd SE19. 081-778 0131. Membership not required. *Open 08.00-22.00 Mon-Fri, 08.00-20.00 Sat, 08.00-18.00 Sun.*

Finsbury Leisure Centre   **2 E4**
Norman St EC1. 071-253 4490. Membership available. *Open 08.00-22.00 Mon-Fri, 09.00-22.00 Sat, 10.00-22.00 Sun.*

Jubilee Sports Centre
Caird St W10. 081-960 9629. Membership available, reduced rates for children. Crèche facilities. *Open 07.00-22.00 Mon-Fri, 08.00-20.00 Sat & Sun.*

Latchmere Sports Centre
Latchmere Rd SW11. 081-871 7470. Membership available, also special family membership scheme. *Open 07.30-21.30 Mon-Sun (to 18.00 Fri).*
Michael Sobell Sports Centre
Hornsey Rd N7. 071-609 2166. Membership available, reduced rates for children. *Open 09.00-23.00 Mon-Fri, 10.00-21.30 Sat & Sun.*
Picketts Lock Sports Centre
Picketts Lock Lane N9. 081-345 6666. Membership available. *Open 10.00-22.00 Mon-Fri, 09.00-21.30 Sat & Sun.*
Queen Mother Sports Centre   **7 C2**
223 Vauxhall Bridge Rd SW1. 071-798 2125. Membership not required. *Open 07.30-19.30 Mon-Thur, to 20.30 Fri, 08.00-17.30 Sat, 09.00-17.15 Sun.*
Swiss Cottage Sports Centre
Winchester Rd NW3. 071-413 6501. Membership not required. *Open 07.30-19.15 Mon & Tue, to 20.30 Wed & Thur, to 16.30 Fri, 09.30-17.00 Sat & Sun.*
YMCA Central   **4 E2**
112 Great Russell St WC1. 071-637 8131. Membership required. *Open 07.00-22.30 Mon-Fri, 10.00-21.00 Sat & Sun.*

★ *Squash* ★ ★ ★ ★ ★ ★ ★ ★ ★ ★ ★ ★ ★ ★

Squash Rackets Association
Westpoint, 33-34 Warple Way, Acton W3. 081-746 1616. For the name of your nearest club with junior membership.

★ *Stamps* ★ ★ ★ ★ ★ ★ ★ ★ ★ ★ ★ ★ ★ ★

If you collect stamps a small corner of London between the Strand and Trafalgar Square is the home of a varied selection of stamp dealers (see *Shopping Guide* on page 135). You'll find everything from first day covers to old, rare and expensive foreign issues.
British Philatelic Trust   **2 D6**
The Secretary, 107 Charterhouse St EC1. 071-251 5040. Provides information on your local club or society, and on exhibitions etc.
National Postal Museum   **5 D2**
King Edward Building, King Edward St EC1. 071-239 5420. Superb display of stamps (see *Museums & Galleries* on page 49).

Stampex
National stamp exhibition held in *Mar* and *Oct* at the Royal Horticultural Society Halls (see *Calendar* on page 17).

★ *Stock Car Racing* ★ ★ ★ ★ ★ ★ ★ ★ ★

Spedeworth International
Wimbledon Stadium, Plough Lane, Wimbledon SW17. 081-946 5361. For information on events.

★ *Sub Aqua* ★ ★ ★ ★ ★ ★ ★ ★ ★ ★ ★

British Sub Aqua Club
Telfords Quay, Ellesmere Port, South Wirral, Cheshire. 051-357 1951. For information on local branches where training courses are run. To join you will have to pass a swimming test and produce a certificate of fitness signed by your doctor.

★ *Swimming* ★ ★ ★ ★ ★ ★ ★ ★ ★ ★ ★

Amateur Swimming Association
Harold Fern House, Derby Sq, Loughborough, Leics. (0509) 230431. Will provide you with details of events, coaching and swimming tests.

There are swimming pools all over London so there's bound to be one near you. The following pools are specially oriented towards children:

Arches Leisure Centre
Trafalgar Rd SE10. 081-317 5000. Goodies include a water flume, a water cannon, volcanic eruptions, a bubbling spring and even a beach area. Crèche and playpens. Family session *Fri evenings. Opening times vary, phone for details.*

Big Splash
Mapleton Rd SW18. 081-871 7675. Paddling pool, diving pool and swimming tank, short-fall waterchute, water features, fountains, play areas and special events. *Open May-Sep 10.00-18.00 Mon-Sun.*

Britannia Leisure Centre
40 Hyde Rd N1. 071-729 4485. Leisure pool in a tropical setting with wave machines, fountains and a huge slide. *Open 09.00-20.45 Mon-Fri, 09.00-17.45 Sat & Sun.*

Fulham Pools
Normand Park, Lillie Rd SW6. 071-385 7628. A great place to splash about. Water chute, wave pool, 25m pool and

teaching pool. Facilities for mothers and young children. Wave pool open for parents and toddlers. *Opening times vary, phone for details.*

Jubilee Sports Centre
Caird St W10. 081-960 9629. Mother and baby sessions, family fun splash on *Sat & Sun afternoons* and a crèche. *Open 07.00-20.00 Mon-Fri, 08.00-16.00 Sat & Sun.*

Thamesmere Pool
Central Way SE28. 081-311 1119. A great pool for children with inflatables, an aqua-skelta and a floom zoom. Crèche. *Opening times vary, phone for details.*

★ Table Tennis ★ ★ ★ ★ ★ ★ ★ ★ ★ ★ ★ ★ ★

English Table Tennis Association
Queensbury House, Havelock Rd, Hastings, East Sussex. (0424) 722525. Gives details of the leagues. South-East region 081-840 4060.

★ Tennis ★ ★ ★ ★ ★ ★ ★ ★ ★ ★ ★ ★ ★ ★ ★

Lawn Tennis Association
Palliser Rd W14. 071-385 2366/071-381 7000. Will give you the name of your local club.
Watching

All England Lawn Tennis & Croquet Club
Church Rd SW19. 081-946 2244. Recorded information: 081-944 1066. For tennis, Wimbledon is the high point in the year. Although the finals are expensive, you can often get cheap tickets for the early days of the competition to watch some of the world's best players. There are also reduced rates to the ground and outside courts, but not Centre and No 1 courts, *after 17.00.*
Another tournament is held at:

Queen's Club
Palliser Rd W14. 071-385 3421. Just before Wimbledon, and you can see many of the stars rather more easily here.

★ Tenpin Bowling ★ ★ ★ ★ ★ ★ ★ ★ ★ ★

British Tenpin Bowling Association
114 Balfour Rd, Ilford, Essex. 081-478 1745. To find out about a club near you.

Lazer Bowl   4 E3
The Trocadero, 13 Coventry St W1. 071-287 8913. Tenpin bowling plus Bowlingo, a more compact version with skiddy black lanes and fluorescent lighting. *Open 10.00-01.00 Mon-Sun.*

★ *Traction Engines* ★ ★ ★ ★ ★ ★ ★ ★ ★ ★

National Traction Engine Trust
Mrs Sylvia Dudley, 12 Hillway, Woburn Sands, Bucks. List of steam rallies and clubs. The junior section is called the Steam Apprentice Club and is for enthusiasts under 21.

★ *Trampolining* ★ ★ ★ ★ ★ ★ ★ ★ ★ ★

British Trampolining Federation
146 College Rd, Harrow, Middx. 081-863 7278. All the information you need to get bouncing.

★ *Volleyball* ★ ★ ★ ★ ★ ★ ★ ★ ★ ★ ★

English Volleyball Association
27 South Rd, West Bridgford, Nottingham, Notts. (0602) 816324. Supplies a list of clubs and fixtures.

★ *Water-skiing* ★ ★ ★ ★ ★ ★ ★ ★ ★ ★

British Water-ski Federation   2 D3
390 City Rd EC1. 071-833 2855. For clubs near you. Residential *summer* courses.

★ *Windsurfing* ★ ★ ★ ★ ★ ★ ★ ★ ★ ★

Windsurfing RYA
Royal Yachting Association, Romsey Rd, Eastleigh, Hants. (0703) 629962. For information, courses and races.

★ *Youth Organisations* ★ ★ ★ ★ ★ ★ ★

Guides Association   4 C6
17-19 Buckingham Palace Rd SW1. 071-834 6242. Girls aged 5-7 become Rainbows, for those aged 7-11 there are Brownie packs and at the age of 10 girls become Girl Guides. From 14-18 they can become Rangers.

London Union of Youth Clubs
64 Camberwell Rd SE5. 071-701 6366. To put you in touch with your local clubs. If you live in Greater London contact the youth and community departments in your local borough. For 7-25 year-olds but mainly 12-21 age group.

NABC – Clubs for Young People
369 Kennington Lane SE11. 071-793 0787. For information about clubs, adventure courses and activity holidays.

Scout Association   3 D5
Baden-Powell House, 65 Queen's Gate SW7. 071-584 7030. Headquarters of the movement. Boys aged 6-8 become Beavers, those aged 8-10½ become Cubs, those aged 10½-15½ become Scouts Troops, 15½-20 year olds can become Venture Scouts. Girls can now also become Scouts at the age of 8-10½.

★ Eating Out

Most restaurants welcome children over 8 and less expensive restaurants are happy to supply children's portions. We have recommended those geared up for the younger ones which offer children's menus and entertainment. Fast food restaurants are plentiful in London and brasseries are also a good place to take children as they have menus which lend themselves to small portions. They are usually open all day and will serve food at any time. Remember that pubs and wine bars are off limits for families with children under 14 unless there is a separate room.

Adams Ribs   7 C1
160 Victoria St SW1. 071-630 5733. American menu offers ribs and burgers. Good value children's menu available for under 10s. *Open 11.30-23.30 Mon-Thur & Sun, 11.30-00.30 Fri & Sat.*

Blue Elephant   6 A5
4-6 Fulham Broadway SW6. 071-385 6595. Thai restaurant with an excellent *Sunday* brunch buffet, offering all-you-can-eat for adults, and a pricing system for kids where children under 4' tall are measured and charged £2 per foot! Clowns entertain while you eat. *Open 12.00-14.30 Mon-Fri & Sun (closed Sat L) & 19.00-00.30 Mon-Sat, to 22.30 Sun.*

Blueprint Café   5 G4
Design Museum, Butler's Wharf SE1. 071-378 7031. On the first floor of the Museum, with a terrace and panoramic views of the Thames. No special menu for children, but they will happily provide small portions. Wide-ranging menu. *Open 12.00-15.00 & 19.00-23.00 Mon-Sat, 12.00-15.30 Sun.*

Caesar's American Restaurant   5 B5
103-107 Waterloo Rd SE1. 071-928 5707. Offers American-style menu, specially for those under 10, at a very reasonable price. *Open 11.30-22.30 Mon-Sat, 11.30-22.00 Sun.*

Café Flo   4 F3
51 St Martin's Lane WC2. 071-836 8289. Special children's menu on *Sat* with the best egg and chips you'll find in this part of town. A good choice for Mums and Dads too. *Open 10.00-23.45 Mon-Sat, 10.00-23.00 Sun.*

Chicago Pizza Pie Factory   **4 C2**
17 Hanover Sq W1. 071-629 2552. Children's menu consists
of either burger or pizza, with ice-cream and a soft drink.
Comic sketches, face painting and magic tricks *13.00-17.00
Sun. Open 11.45-23.30 Mon-Sat, 12.00-22.30 Sun.*

Chuen Cheng Ku   **4 E3**
17 Wardour St W1. 071-437 1398. Large, busy Chinese
restaurant. They do not cater specifically for children but
have high chairs for those that need them. Supposed to
have one of Chinatown's longest menus. *Open 11.00-24.00
Mon-Sat, 11.00-23.15 Sun.*

Deals   **6 C6**
Chelsea Harbour SW3. 071-352 5887. A friendly, modern
restaurant with a special family day on *Sun;* magician and
face painting from *12.00-15.00.* Children's menu with burgers, fish fingers and fries. *Open 12.00-23.00 Mon-Thur,
12.00-23.30 Fri-Sat, 12.00-22.00 Sun.*

Down Mexico Way   **4 D3**
25 Swallow St W1. 071-437 9895. A Spanish restaurant with
an authentic flavour. High chairs available and they will do
small portions for children on request from their interesting
menu. *Open 12.00-23.45 Mon-Sat, 12.00-22.30 Sun.*

Garfunkel's   **4 C2**
265 Regent St W1. 071-629 1870. Family restaurant with
branches all round the West End. American-style grub with
a separate menu for kids. *Open 11.30-23.30 Mon-Sat,
12.00-23.30 Sun.*

Geales Fish Restaurant   **3 B4**
2 Farmer St W8. 071-727 7969. Must be one of the best
fish and chip shops in town. Large choice of fish, from trout
to shark, all bought daily from Billingsgate market. Reduced
price children's portions on request. Also high chairs and
booster seats available. Definitely a place for the whole
family. *Open 12.00-15.00 & 18.00-23.00 Tue-Sat. Closed
Sun & Mon.*

Henry J Bean's Bar & Grill
195-197 King's Rd SW3. 071-352 9255.   **6 E3**
Open 12.00-23.00 Mon-Sat, to 22.00 Sun.
54 Abingdon Rd W8. 071-937 3339.   **3 B6**
Open 11.45-22.30 Mon-Sat, 12.00-22.00 Sun.
Modelled on a typical American grill. SW3 branch has a huge
garden with a play area; W8 branch has pinball tables.

McDonald's
57 Haymarket SW1. 071-930 9302.   **4 E3**
108-110 Kensington High St W8. 071-937 3705.   **3 C5**

2-4 Marble Arch W2. 071-402 6297.   **4 A3**
8-10 Oxford St W1. 071-636 4350.   **4 E2**
35 Strand WC2. 071-930 7530.   **4 F3**
155 Victoria St SW1. 071-828 6911.   **7 C1**
Branches all over London. The above is only a small
selection. Famous swift service and efficient, clean, modern surroundings. Mostly take-away but you can sit down if
you want. Good hamburger and chips, thick, creamy milk-
shakes and fruit pies. All restaurants have high chairs and
most will take bookings for children's parties. Phone your
local branch for details. Majority of branches *open 11.00-
23.00 Mon-Sun.*

My Old Dutch   **4 F2**
131 High Holborn WC1. 071-242 5200. Huge pancakes
with 67 different types of filling. The pancakes are thin
so even the biggest aren't a problem to finish. *Open
11.00-23.00 Mon & Tue, 11.30-23.30 Wed-Sat, 10.30-22.30
Sun.*

Pappagalli's Pizza   **4 D3**
7-9 Swallow St W1. 071-734 5182. Large, lively deep-dish
pizza restaurant. All sorts of pastas and pizzas on offer with
scrummy Italian ice-cream to follow. Small portions of pasta
on request. Booster seats. *Open 12.00-23.00 Mon-Sat.
Closed Sun.*

Pizza Hut   **4 E2**
3 Cambridge Circus WC2. 071-379 4655. Pizza chain
with many branches throughout London. Children's menu,
pizza buffet (eat as much as you can!), play packs and
collectable toys. *Open 12.00-24.00 Mon-Fri & Sun, 11.00-
24.00 Sat.*

Rock Island Diner   **4 E3**
2nd Floor, London Pavilion, Piccadilly W1. 071-287 5500.
Truly American 50s and 60s diner complete with dancing
waitresses and its own radio station, WRID. Grilled
sandwiches, burgers, hot dogs, salads and chocolate
brownies with hot fudge sauce and ice-cream. Children's
menu *until 17.00.* Children under 10 eat free from *12.00-
17.00 Sat & Sun* when accompanied by an adult who
orders a main course. Competitions and prizes, DJs,
*12.00-23.00 Sat & Sun. Open 12.00-23.30 Mon-Sat, to
23.00 Sun.*

Roxy Café Cantina   **2 D2**
297 Upper St N1. 071-226 5746. Tex-Mex restaurant
wonderfully suited for families. Tacos, enchiladas and
tostadas can be served as side orders for children, or a
special children's set menu of burgers, chips and a drink.
Open 12.00-24.00 Mon-Sat, 12.30-23.00 Sun.

Selfridges Food Garden Café   **4 B2**
Oxford St W1. 071-629 1234. A useful one to remember if
in Oxford Street. Burgers and pasta in half portions. *Open
09.30-18.45 Mon-Sat (to 19.45 Thur).*
Le Shop   **6 D4**
329 King's Rd SW3. 071-352 3891. Typical Breton
crêperie, very friendly and always busy. Crêpes are
delicious, light and hot – sweet or savoury in lots of
combinations. Reduced priced kids portions. Baby chairs
and books for children. *Open 12.00-24.00 Mon-Fri, 10.30-
24.00 Sat & Sun.*
Signor Zilli   **4 E3**
41 Dean St W1. 071-734 3924. Family *Sunday* lunches of
either Italian food or traditional roast. Entertainment *13.00-
15.00 Sun* can be tableside magicians, puppets, Punch and
Judy shows, kids disco. *Open 12.00-15.00 & 18.00-23.30
Mon-Sun (closed Sat lunchtimes).*

Smollensky's Balloon   4 D4
1 Dover St W1. 071-491 1199. Enterprising family restaurant. Excellent international menu with special junior steaks, hamburgers, chicken nuggets, fish and chips and pasta dishes. Look out for the peanut butter cheese-cake. Entertainments on *Sat & Sun afternoons 13.00-15.00,* including a Punch & Judy show, magicians, clowns and story-tellers. *Open 12.00-24.00 Mon-Sat, 12.00-22.30 Sun.*

Texas Lone Star Saloon   6 C2
154 Gloucester Rd SW7. 071-370 5625. Tex-Mex restaurant done out like a saloon. Wild West videos. Ribs, burgers and frankfurters. Open *12.00-23.30 Sun-Wed, 12.00-00.30 Thur-Sat.*

Thank God It's Fridays   4 F3
6 Bedford St W2. 071-379 0585. Large, loud and lively diner, serving American and Tex-Mex food. Crunchy potato skins are a favourite. Smaller portions of the regular menu available as well as special children's hamburgers. High chairs and booster seats. Magician and face painting *Sun afternoon. Open 12.00-23.30 Mon-Sun.*

Tootsies
115 Notting Hill Gate W11. 071-727 6562.   3 B4
120 Holland Park Ave W11. 071-229 8567.
177 New King's Rd SW6. 071-736 4023.
Small chain of attractive American restaurants, serving steaks, burgers, sandwiches and vegetarian dishes. The atmosphere is cheerful and easy-going. Special children's menu is cheap and healthy. Booster chairs and high chairs. *Open 12.00-23.30 Mon-Thur, 12.00-24.00 Fri, 11.00-24.00 Sat, 11.00-23.00 Sun.*

Uncle Ian's Deli Diner
8-10 Monkville Parade NW11. 081-458 3493. Extremely popular for family lunches. Excellent children's menu and free lollipops. *Open 09.00-23.30 Mon-Sun (closes at 16.00 on Fri).*

Victoria & Albert Museum   6 D1
New Restaurant, Henry Cole Wing, Cromwell Rd SW7. 071-938 8358. A good place to remember if you're doing the museums. Good salads and hot dishes. High chairs and children's portions available. *Open 10.00-17.00 Tue-Sun, 12.00-17.00 Mon.*

TEA ▰▰▰▰▰▰▰▰▰▰▰▰▰▰▰▰▰

Fortnum & Mason   4 D4
181 Piccadilly W1. 071-734 8040. Afternoon tea in the Fountain Restaurant and St James Restaurant. Scones, sandwiches, cakes etc. High chairs available. Tea served from *15.00-18.00 Mon-Sat* in the Fountain Restaurant and *15.00-17.30 Mon-Sat* in St James Restaurant.

Harrods Georgian Restaurant 3 G6
Knightsbridge SW1. 071-730 1234. Buffet tea with bread and butter, scones, cakes and pastries accompanied by a pianist. High chairs available. Tea served from *15.45-17.15 Mon-Sat.*

Heal's Restaurant 4 E1
196 Tottenham Court Rd W1. 071-636 1666. On the first floor of the store. Sandwiches, scones, gateaux, cakes. High chairs available. Tea served from *15.00-17.30 Mon-Sat.*

Maison Sagne 1 C6
105 Marylebone High St W1. 071-935 6240. Traditional tea shop with its own bakery and delicious pâtisserie. *Open 08.00-20.00 Mon-Fri, 08.00-18.00 Sat, 09.00-18.00 Sun.*

Masserellas 4 D3
188-196 Regent St W1. 071-734 3161. On the lower ground floor of Hamleys toy shop. Hot, healthy dishes like lasagne, chilli and soup. Also sandwiches, cakes and ice creams. Plenty of space for prams, pushchairs and shopping. *Open 10.00-18.30 Mon-Wed, to 20.00 Thur, to 19.00 Fri, 09.30-19.00 Sat, 12.00-18.00 Sun.*

Muffin Man 3 C6
12 Wright's Lane W8. 071-937 6652. Breakfast, morning coffee, light lunches and a range of set teas: Devon, and 'Muffin Man' traditional. *Open 08.00-17.30 Mon-Sat.*

Pâtisserie Valerie 4 E3
44 Old Compton St W1. 071-437 3466. Soho pâtisserie with tea, coffee and hot chocolate. Excellent cream cakes and sandwiches. *Open 08.00-20.00 Mon-Fri, 08.00-19.00 Sat, 10.00-17.30 Sun.*

ICE-CREAM

Baskin-Robbins
Empire Cinema, Leicester Sq WC2. 071-734 8222. 4 E3
Plaza Cinema, Lower Regent St W1. 071-930 0144. 4 E3
31 amazing flavours to choose from. If you can't decide you can always ask for a sample. *Open 11.00-23.00 Mon-Sun.*

Haagen Dazs
75 Hampstead High St NW3. 071-794 0646. *Open 10.00-23.00.*
138a King's Rd SW3. 071-823 9326. *Open 10.00-23.00.* 6 F3
The Piazza, Covent Garden WC2. 071-240 0436. 4 F3
Open 10.00-23.00.
Leicester Sq WC2. 071-287 9577. 4 E3
Open 10.00-24.00 Mon-Sun, to 01.00 Fri & Sat.
16 flavours of scrumptious full cream American ice-cream.

Marine Ices 1 C1
8 Haverstock Hill NW3. 071-485 3132. Reputedly the best ice-cream in London. 18 flavours of ice-cream, real fruit sorbets, knickerbocker glories and peach melbas. *Open 10.30-22.45 Mon-Sat, 11.00-19.00 Sun.*

★ *Shopping Guide*

London is one of the best cities in the world for shopping and whatever your taste you will find what you want somewhere.

★ *Arts & Crafts* ★ ★ ★ ★ ★ ★ ★ ★ ★ ★

Bead Shop   4 F2
43 Neal St WC2. 071-240 0931. Bits and pieces to make your own bangles, necklaces and earrings. The beads come in every conceivable shape, size and colour so there's plenty to choose from. Also sells the essentials like string, clasps, earring fittings and so on. *Open 13.00-18.00 Mon, 10.30-18.00 Tue-Fri, 11.30-17.00 Sat.*

Candle Shop   4 F3
30 The Market, Covent Garden Market WC2. 071-836 9815. Buy a candle-making kit here and look at the candles on display for ideas. *Open 10.00-20.00 Mon-Sat, 10.00-19.00 Sun.*

Most of the large department stores in London are well equipped to deal with shopping for the family and provide a separate mother and baby room.
The following provide facilities for mothers and children:

Debenhams   4 C2
Oxford St W1. 071-580 3000.
Hamleys   4 D3
188-196 Regent St W1. 071-734 8040.
Harrods   3 G6
Knightsbridge SW1. 071-730 1234.
John Lewis   4 C2
Oxford St W1. 071-629 7711.
Peter Jones   6 F2
Sloane Sq SW1. 071-730 3434.
Selfridges   4 B2
Oxford St W1. 071-629 1234.
Trocadero Centre   4 E3
Piccadilly Circus W1. 071-439 1791.

Reward Clay Glaze 7 B6
8-10 Ingate Place SW8. 071-720 0050. For the young potter a choice of 20 clays, materials and equipment as well as tools, kilns and glazes. *Open 09.00-17.00 Mon-Sat.*

Hobby Horse 6 C4
15-17 Langton St SW10. 071-351 1913. An Aladdin's cave of beads to create your own designer jewellery. Essentials, like thread, clasps and earring fittings can be bought here too. *Open 10.00-17.30 Mon-Sat.*

London Graphics Centre 4 F2
107 Long Acre WC2. 071-240 0095. All sorts of bits and pieces for drawing and graphics, including an amazing selection of coloured papers. *Open 09.00-18.00 Mon-Fri, 10.30-18.00 Sat.*

Paperchase 4 E1
213 Tottenham Court Rd W1. 071-580 8496. Every sort of paper an artist could possibly want in millions of colours and textures. *Open 10.00-18.00 Mon, 09.00-18.00 Tue-Sat (to 19.00 Thur).*

Reeves Dryad 3 B5
178 Kensington High St W8. 071-937 5370. The place to go for art materials: all kinds of oils, water-colours, brushes and pencils to choose from. *Open 09.00-17.30 Mon-Fri, 09.30-17.30 Sat.*

Ries Wools 4 F1
8 Sicilian Ave WC1. 071-242 7721. A knitting and tapestry shop selling Rowan, Annabel Fox and Jaeger knitting yarns. *Open 10.00-17.00 Mon-Wed, 10.00-19.00 Thur, 10.00-14.30 Fri. Closed Sat.*

WHI Tapestry Shop 7 A3
85 Pimlico Rd SW1. 071-730 5366. Everything for needle-point from thimbles and scissors to painted tapestry canvases. Also a making-up service. *Open 09.30-17.00 Mon-Fri.*

Winsor & Newton 4 E2
51 Rathbone Place W1. 071-636 4231. Well-made paints, papers and brushes. They stock well over 100 oil paints including half-a-dozen shades of white. *Open 09.00-17.30 Mon-Fri, 09.00-17.00 Sat.*

★ *Bicycles* ★ ★ ★ ★ ★ ★ ★ ★ ★ ★ ★ ★ ★

Before you rush off to one of the shops listed below, it's worth looking at the bicycle sections in some of the big department stores like Harrods and John Lewis.

Bike Peddlers 2 B5
50 Calthorpe St WC1. 071-278 0551. Plenty of bikes to

choose from in this well-known shop, plus spares and repairs. *Open 09.00-14.30 & 15.30-18.00 Mon-Fri, 10.00-13.00 Sat.*

Chamberlain   **1 D1**
71-77 Kentish Town Rd NW1. 071-485 3983. Wide range of makes and sizes in stock for all ages. Cycle hire and repair service offered. *Open 08.30-18.00 Mon-Sat.*

Cycle Logical   **4 D1**
136-138 New Cavendish St W1. 071-631 5060. Stockists of Muddy Fox mountain bikes and accessories and also strong, durable clothing suitable for off-road expeditions. A custom wheel-building service is also offered. *Open 09.00-18.00 Mon-Sat, 12.00-17.00 Sun.*

Kensington Cycle Centre
69 Golborne Rd W10. 081-960 0444. Good, reliable bike shop, mostly second-hand stock. Full safety check here if you're worried about your bike's road worthiness. *Open 10.00-17.00 Mon-Sat (to 13.00 Thur).*

South Bank Bicycles
194 Wandsworth Rd SW8. 071-622 3069. This shop caters for the everyday cyclist with a good range of road bikes, wet weather gear and a range of spares. Also mountain bikes, racing bikes and a good selection of specialist clothing. *Open 09.00-19.00 Tue-Fri, 10.00-17.00 Sat.*

W F Holdsworth
132 Lower Richmond Rd SW15. 081-788 1060. Rows of new and used bikes for toddlers and teenagers. Mainly stocks Raleigh, Dawes, Specialised and Ridgeback. Good for cycling equipment and repairs. *Open 09.00-18.00 Tue, Wed & Sat, 09.00-19.00 Thur, 09.00-17.30 Fri.*

★ *Books, Maps & Comics* ★ ★ ★ ★ ★ ★ ★

Books for Children
97 Wandsworth Bridge Rd SW6. 071-384 1821. A delightful bookshop with a wide range of children's books. *Open 10.00-18.00 Mon, 09.30-18.00 Tue-Fri, 09.30-17.30 Sat.*

Children's Book Centre   **3 B6**
237 Kensington High St W8. 071-937 7497. The largest children's bookshop in the country with some 30,000 titles. Also sells videos and toys. In the *school hols* there are story-telling sessions. *Open 09.30-18.30 Mon-Sat (to 19.00 Thur). Open occasional Sundays 12.30-18.00 ring for details.*

Children's Bookshop
29 Fortis Green Rd N10. 081-444 5500. Specialist children's

bookshop with knowledgeable and helpful staff. Programme of events throughout the year, plus story-telling in *summer*. *Open 09.15-17.45 Mon-Fri, 09.15-17.30 Sat, 12.00-17.00 Sun.*

Comic Showcase   4 F2

76 Neal St WC2. 071-240 3664. Lots of whizzy reading for the whole family. *Open 10.00-18.00 Mon-Wed & Sun, 10.00-19.00 Thur & Fri, 09.30-19.00 Sat.*

Dillons   3 C5

48-52 Kensington High St W8. 071-938 2228. Very well-stocked book store, with a wide variety of adult and children's books. Other branches. *Open 09.30-20.00 Mon-Sat, 12.00-19.00 Sun.*

Forbidden Planet   4 E2

71 New Oxford St WC1. 071-836 4179. Large bookshop combining the science fiction, fantasy, horror and comic worlds. *Open 10.00-18.00 Mon-Wed & Sat, 10.00-19.00 Thur & Fri.*

Foyles   4 E2

113-119 Charing Cross Rd WC2. 071-437 5660. The largest bookshop of them all with a well-stocked children's section. *Open 09.00-18.00 Mon-Sat (to 19.00 Thur).*

Geographia Map Shop   5 C2

58 Ludgate Hill EC4. 071-248 3554. Extensive selection of maps and guides as well as a variety of atlases and globes. *Open 09.00-17.15 Mon-Fri. Closed Sat.*

Gosh   4 F1

39 Great Russell St WC1. 071-636 1011. All the comics you can think of, plus plenty you will never have heard of! *Open 10.00-18.00 Mon-Sun (to 19.00 Thur & Fri).*

Hatchards   4 D3

187 Piccadilly W1. 071-439 9921. A good stock of books including a comprehensive children's section upstairs. The search department will track down titles for you. *Open 09.00-18.00 Mon-Fri, 09.30-18.00 Tue & Sat.*

Marchpane   4 F3

16 Cecil Court WC2. 071-836 8661. A stunning collection of illustrated children's books. Early *Alice in Wonderland* books and first editions, plus *Just William* second editions, Beatrix Potter accessories. *Open 10.30-18.30 Mon-Sat.*

Puffin Bookshop   4 F3

1 Covent Garden Market WC2. 071-379 6465. Large stock of children's books, including the full Puffin range. Adult titles downstairs. *Open 10.00-18.30 Mon-Sat, 10.30-18.30 Tue, 12.00-18.00 Sun.*

Sportspages   4 E2
94-96 Charing Cross Rd WC2. 071-240 9604. Sports bookshop covering all aspects of sport and fitness. Also stocks
magazines and videos. *Open 09.30-19.00 Mon-Sat.*

Stanfords   4 F3
12-14 Long Acre WC2. 071-836 1321. World's largest map
and travel bookshop. Amongst the vast range of travel
books you will also find wall maps of the world, ancient
plans of towns and globes. *Open 10.00-18.00 Mon-Sat,
09.00-19.00 Tue.*

Waterstone's   3 B6
193 Kensington High St W8. 071-937 8432. Huge range of
books including children's section. Other branches. *Open
09.30-21.00 Mon-Fri, 09.30-19.00 Sat, 11.00-18.00 Sun.*

★ *Camping* ★ ★ ★ ★ ★ ★ ★ ★ ★ ★ ★ ★ ★

Adventure Shops   4 F3
14 Southampton St WC2. 071-836 8541. Caters for everyone
from trekkers to skiers. Has a good selection of Karrimor ruck-
sacks, tents, Tenson jackets for very wet occasions and ski
boots. Also a good maps and guides section. You can join the
YHA on the spot here. *Open 10.00-18.00 Mon-Wed, 10.00-
19.00 Thur & Fri, 09.00-18.30 Sat.*

Blacks   4 E2
53 Rathbone Place W1. 071-636 6645. Specialists in climbing and mountaineering and probably the most versatile
camping shop in London with everything from feather-
weight airbeds to the ultimate tent. *Open 09.30-18.00 Mon-
Fri, to 19.00 Thur, 10.00-17.30 Sat.*

Camping & Outdoor Centres Scout Shops   4 C6
27 Buckingham Palace Rd SW1. 071-834 6007. Everything
you need for a hardy week outdoors. Stocks kit especially
for camping. *Open 09.00-17.30 Mon-Sat.*

Guides Association Shop   4 C6
17 Buckingham Palace Rd SW1. 071-834 6242. Good range
of tents and camping accessories for weekends away. *Open
09.00-17.30 Mon-Fri, to 13.00 Sat.*

★ *Clothes & Shoes* ★ ★ ★ ★ ★ ★ ★ ★ ★ ★

For everyday wear the best buys are in the chain stores and
department stores but you can find stylish designer clothes
for even the youngest children. There are also a number of
second-hand children's clothes shops where you can find
nearly-new and outgrown clothes.

Anthea Moore Ede 3 D6

16 Victoria Grove W8. 071-584 8826. Traditional baby's and children's clothes in natural fibres, including beautiful hand-smocked dresses. Stocks clothes for 0-14s. *Open 09.00-17.00 Mon-Fri, 10.00-13.00 Sat.*

Buckle My Shoe 4 B2

19 St Christopher's Place W1. 071-935 5589. Fun and fashionable shoes for 0-8 year-olds. Everything from baseball boots to black patent pumps. *Open 10.00-18.00 Mon-Sat (to 19.00 Thur).*

C & A 4 B2

501-509 Oxford St W1. 071-629 7272. Good selection of inexpensive clothes for those under 16, especially trendy sports kit. Other branches. *Open 09.30-19.00 Mon-Sat (to 20.00 Thur).*

Clark's 4 B2

437 Oxford St W1. 071-629 9609. Good, well-known children's shoe store stocking Clark's shoes. Full measuring facilities to get shoes which fit properly. Other branches. *Open 09.30-18.30 Mon-Wed, to 20.00 Thur, to 19.00 Fri, to 18.00 Sat.*

Confiture 6 D2

19 Harrington Rd SW7. 071-581 3432. Full of original and imaginative clothes for 0-12s. Mostly chic and colourful French, Spanish and Italian designs. *Open 10.00-18.30 Mon-Fri, 10.30-18.00 Sat.*

The Gap 4 D3

144-146 Regent St W1. 071-287 5095. All-American denims, sweatshirts and cotton knits for children from 2-13 years. *Open 09.30-19.00 Mon-Sat (to 20.00 Thur).*

Grant Shoes 3 G5

24-26 Brompton Rd SW3. 071-581 8661. A wide variety of children's shoes from black patents to the latest designs. Stocks up to size 8. *Open 10.00-18.30 Mon-Sat (to 19.00 Wed).*

Hennes 4 D2

Oxford Circus W1. 071-493 4004. Vast range of casual, fun clothes for children including romper suits, T-shirts and sweatshirts. High fashion at budget prices. *Open 10.00-18.45 Mon-Fri (to 20.00 Thur), 09.15-18.15 Sat.*

Humla 4 D2

4 Marlborough Court, Newburgh St W1. 071-434 0385. Specialises in original and fun knitwear for 0-12s. Colourful range of mix 'n' match garments. Good for gift ideas too. *Open 10.30-18.00 Mon-Sat.*

Instep   1 A3
45 St John's Wood High St NW8. 071-722 7634. For toddlers to teenagers with feet up to size 8. Stocks school shoes, fashion shoes, ballet pumps, wellies and Start-Rite shoes. Fitting service. Free entertainment of video cartoons while you wait. *Open 09.30-17.30 Mon-Sat.*

Just Outgrown
99 Devonshire Rd W4. 081-995 5405. Nearly-new and new clothes. Everything from designer babywear to age 12 jeans. Ever-changing stock. Also cots, toys, prams and maternitywear. *Open 10.00-16.00 Tue-Fri, 10.00-13.00 Sat.*

Laura Ashley   4 D2
256-8 Regent St W1. 071-437 9760. Pastoral prints on skirts, dungarees, shirts and Victorian-style party dresses. Just right for the little ones with sailor suits and pinafores but a bit square for teenagers. Other branches. *Open 10.00-18.30 Mon & Tue, to 19.00 Wed & Fri, to 20.00 Thur, 09.30-19.00 Sat.*

Liberty   4 D2
210-222 Regent St W1. 071-734 1234. Beautiful clothes in beautiful print materials. *Open 09.30-18.00 Mon, Tue, Fri & Sat, 10.00-18.00 Wed, 09.00-19.30 Thur.*

Little Perishers   2 D1
139 Upper St N1. 071-226 3344. Original and high quality children's togs, but on the pricey side. Downstairs is a nursery equipment section selling some of the more well-known names. *Open 10.00-18.00 Mon-Sat.*

Marks & Spencer   4 B2
458 Oxford St W1. 071-935 7954. Largest branch and normally the first one to get the new ranges. One of the best for value for children's clothes and shoes. *Open 09.00-19.00 Mon-Wed & Sat, 09.00-20.00 Thur & Fri.*

Mothercare   4 B2
461 Oxford St W1. 071-629 6621. Good quality everyday clothes at reasonable prices. Co-ordinated tops and bottoms as well as accessories for babies and children up to 11. Other branches. *Open 09.00-19.00 Mon-Sat, to 20.00 Thur.*

Next   3 C5
54-60 Kensington High St W8. 071-938 4211. Next department store with a special section called NBG full of trendy children's wear: thick cotton tracksuits, duffle coats and a small range of interesting shoes. Other branches. *Open 10.00-19.00 Mon-Fri, 10.00-18.00 Sat.*

Oshkosh B'Gosh
17-19 King's Rd SW3. 071-730 1341. American childrenswear for the under 12s. *Open 09.30-18.00 Mon-Sat, 10.00-19.00 Wed.*

012   **4 C3**
522 Oxford St W1. 071-491 1238. Junior version of the ever popular Benetton. Colourful, up-to-date Italian casual clothes. Other branches. *Open 09.30-18.30 Mon-Sat (to 20.00 Thur).*

Please Mum   **4 C2**
69 New Bond St W1. 071-493 5880. Expensive, dressy, mainly Italian clothes for new-born babies to 14 year-olds. Fancy party costumes that can be made to order. Branch at 15 Orchard St W1. *Open 09.45-19.00 Mon-Sat (to 20.00 Thur).*

Pollyanna
811 Fulham Rd SW6. 071-731 0673. Beautifully designed, practical but unusual clothes for boys and girls up to age 8. *Open 09.30-19.30 Mon-Sat.*

Russell & Bromley   **6 F2**
64-66 King's Rd SW3. 071-584 5445. Vast range of shoes for children – starting at size 2. *Open 09.30-18.00 Mon, Fri & Sat, 10.00-18.00 Tue & Thur, 10.00-19.00 Wed.*

Small Change
25 Carnegie House, Well Rd NW3. 071-794 3043. Only the best second-hand clothes from babywear to early teens. Clothes are taken on a sale or return basis. *Open 09.00-17.00 Mon-Fri (to 18.00 Tue), 10.00-17.00 Sat.*

Sunflower
36 Union Court, Richmond, Surrey. 081-948 5792. A nearly-new shop filled with good quality children's clothes at half the original ticket price. *Open 10.00-15.00 Mon-Fri, 10.00-13.00 Sat.*

White House   **4 C2**
51-52 New Bond St W1. 071-629 3521. Children's tailored clothes, mostly French and Italian imports in traditional styles: classic smocks, velvet-collared coats and sailor suits. *Open 09.00-17.30 Mon-Fri, 09.00-13.00 Sat.*

Woolworths   **3 F2**
168 Edgware Rd W2. 071-723 2391. Exclusive stockists of Ladybird clothes. Very reasonably-priced and well-made selection of children's clothes. Other branches. *Open 09.00-19.00 Mon-Fri, 09.00-18.00 Sat, 11.00-17.00 Sun.*

★ *Computers* ★ ★ ★ ★ ★ ★ ★ ★ ★ ★ ★ ★

Lots of high-street chain stores now sell computers but their selection of software can be limited. The heart and soul of London's computer world is Tottenham Court Road (**4 E1**) where dozens of shops sell computers, printers and electronic gear.

Centre Point Software   4 E2
20-21 St Giles High St, Centre Point WC2. 071-836 0599.
Huge selection of computer software including all the top
computer games. *Open 09.00-18.00 Mon-Fri, 10.00-18.00 Sat.*

★ *Dance* ★ ★ ★ ★ ★ ★ ★ ★ ★ ★ ★ ★ ★ ★ ★

Freed's   4 F3
94 St Martin's Lane WC2. 071-240 0432. Beautifully made
dance shoes as well as dance wear: modern and traditional,
tutus and leotards. All moderately priced. *Open 09.00-17.15
Mon-Fri, 09.00-15.30 Sat.*

★ *Furniture & Furnishings* ★ ★ ★ ★ ★ ★

Dragons of Walton Street   6 F1
23 Walton St SW3. 071-589 5007. Sells nursery furniture by
Rosie Fisher, who designed Prince William's nursery. All
furniture here is beautifully made. *Open 09.30-17.30 Mon-
Fri, 10.00-17.00 Sat.*
Mothercare   4 B2
461 Oxford St W1. 071-629 6621. A complete range of
baby basics like cot blankets, slings, simple wooden nursery
furniture, carrycots, prams and so on. Also strong on child
safety items like car safety harnesses, cooker guards and
safety covers for electric sockets. Other branches. *Open
09.30-19.00 Mon-Sat.*

★ *Hairdressing* ★ ★ ★ ★ ★ ★ ★ ★ ★ ★ ★ ★

Most hairdressers have assistants who will do children's
hair so when you book your own appointment it is worth-
while asking if you can take your child as well.

Harrods   3 G6
Knightsbridge SW1. 071-730 1234. There is a special hair-
dressing department for children. *Open 09.00-18.00 Mon,
Tue & Sat, 09.00-19.00 Wed & Fri, 10.00-19.00 Thur.*

★ *Kites* ★ ★ ★ ★ ★ ★ ★ ★ ★ ★ ★ ★ ★ ★ ★

High as a Kite
153 Stoke Newington Church St N16. 071-275 8799. Sells
single line, box and stunt kites. Also frisbees, boomerangs
and juggling equipment. *Open 09.30-18.30 Mon-Sat.*
The Balloon & Kite Emporium
613 Garratt Lane SW18. 081-946 5962. A fantastic range of

kites: all shapes and sizes for all ages. Also a wonderful variety of balloons, including helium ones with your name on and special birthday balloons. *Open 09.00-18.00 Mon-Sat.*

Kite Store 4 F2
48 Neal St WC2. 071-836 1666. Kites of every imaginable design as well as piles of frisbees and boomerangs. They also have simple, colourful kites you can assemble yourself, as well as brightly-designed ones. Mail order service. Phone for details. *Open 10.00-18.00 Mon-Fri (to 19.00 Thur), 10.30-18.00 Sat.*

★ *Magic, Jokes & Tricks* ★ ★ ★ ★ ★ ★ ★

Davenports Joke Shop 4 F4
7 Charing Cross Underground Shopping Concourse WC2. 071-836 0408. Davenports has been going since 1898. Sells jokes, tricks, puzzles, practical jokes – some at pocket money prices. Plus elaborate tricks for Mums and Dads. *Open 10.15-17.30 Mon-Fri, 09.30-16.30 Sat. Closed Sun.*

★ *Models* ★ ★ ★ ★ ★ ★ ★ ★ ★ ★ ★ ★ ★

Beatties 4 F1
202 High Holborn WC1. 071-405 6285. Train sets, train components and railway landscapes with models from Hornby, Lima and Marklin. Also lots of radio-controlled toys. Knowledgeable staff. Other branches. *Open 10.00-18.00 Mon, 09.00-18.00 Tue-Fri, 09.00-17.30 Sat.*

Comet Miniatures
46-48 Lavender Hill SW11. 071-228 3702. Warehouse and shop specialising in rare and obsolete aircraft kits. Martian war machines, space rocket kits, futuristic Thunderbirds rockets. *Open 09.30-17.30 Mon-Sat.*

Hamleys 4 D3
188-196 Regent St W1. 071-734 3161. Plenty of models to be found on all floors of this large store. *Open 10.00-18.30 Mon-Wed, 10.00-20.00 Thur, 10.00-19.00 Fri, 09.30-19.00 Sat, 12.00-18.00 Sun.*

St Martin's Accessories 4 F3
95 St Martin's Lane WC2. 071-836 9742. Model car specialist. *Open 09.30-18.00 Mon-Fri, 10.00-16.00 Sat.*

W & H Models   **4 B1**
14 New Cavendish St W1. 071-935 5810. Sells the more
expensive train sets, scale models and kits, for the serious
collector. *Open 09.00-18.00 Mon-Sat, to 19.00 Thur.*

★ *Music* ★ ★ ★ ★ ★ ★ ★ ★ ★ ★ ★ ★ ★ ★ ★

If you're looking for an instrument, the best shops to browse
in are along London's own 'Tin Pan Alley' – Denmark Street
WC2 (**4 E2**). The whole area around here, especially along
Charing Cross Road and Shaftesbury Avenue, is dotted with
shops selling instruments and sheet music.

INSTRUMENTS & SHEET MUSIC ▬▬▬

Andy's Guitar Centre & Workshop   **4 E2**
27 Denmark St WC2. 071-916 5080. New and second-
hand electric guitars. Workshop at the back where
guitars are made and repaired. Shop *open 10.00-22.00
Mon-Sat, 12.30-18.30 Sun.* Workshop *open 10.00-17.00
Tue-Sat.*
Bluthner   **4 C3**
8 Berkeley Sq W1. 071-753 0533. World-famous pianos.
Open 09.00-17.00 Mon-Fri, 10.00-17.00 Sat.
Boosey & Hawkes   **4 C2**
295 Regent St W1. 071-580 2060. Manufactures a whole
range of brass and woodwind instruments. Sells instrumental
accessories, music and books, but no instruments from
here. *Open 09.00-18.00 Mon-Fri, 10.00-16.00 Sat.*

Schott & Co **4 D2**
48 Great Marlborough St W1. 071-437 1246. Sheet music and scores. *Open 09.00-17.30 Mon-Fri.*

J & A Beare **4 E2**
7 Broadwick St W1. 071-437 1449. Fine old violins, violas and cellos. Also restorers of musical instruments. *Open 09.00-12.15 & 13.30-17.00 Mon-Fri.*

Paxman **4 F2**
116 Long Acre WC2. 071-240 3642. One of the most famous horn makers in the world; they sell all types, both new and second-hand. Sheet music and repairs. *Open 09.30-17.30 Mon-Fri, 10.00-17.00 Sat.*

Professional Percussion
205 Kentish Town Rd NW5. 071-485 0822. Vast selection of drums, drum kits and other percussion instruments. Accessories and second-hand equipment too. *Open 10.00-18.00 Mon-Sat.*

Steinway and Sons **4 C2**
44 Marylebone Lane, Wigmore St W1. 071-487 3391. One of the most famous makes of pianos on sale here. Steinways have been made since 1853. *Open 09.00-17.30 Mon-Fri, 10.30-16.30 Sat.*

TW Howarth **1 C6**
31 Chiltern St W1. 071-935 2407. Manufacturers of oboes d'amore and cor anglais. Woodwind specialists. Music accessories, woodwind repairs. *Open 10.00-17.30 Mon-Fri, 10.00-15.00 Sat.*

RECORDS, CASSETTES & COMPACT DISCS ▮▮▮▮▮

HMV **4 D2**
150 Oxford St W1. 071-631 3423. Comprehensive assortment of music including children's music, Walt Disney sound tracks and bedtime stories. Games centre. Other branches. *Open 09.30-19.00 Mon-Sat (to 20.00 Thur & Fri).*

Tower Records **4 E3**
1 Piccadilly Circus W1. 071-439 2500. The 'greatest record store in the world', this prime-site shop on four floors offers the full spectrum of sounds from golden oldies to opera, jazz and hard rock. Stories on tape and record for children and special Disney, Sesame Street and Winnie the Pooh selections. *Open 09.00-24.00 Mon-Sat, 11.00-22.00 Sun.*

Virgin Megastore **4 E2**
14-16 Oxford St W1. 071-631 1234. Another competitor for the biggest and best. Progressive and popular music, blues,

jazz, classical – almost everything at good discounts. Good choice of children's music and all sorts of stories on tape and record. *Open 09.30-20.00 Mon-Sat.*

★ *Posters* ★ ★ ★ ★ ★ ★ ★ ★ ★ ★ ★ ★ ★ ★ ★

Athena   **4 D2**
119-121 Oxford St W1. 071-734 3383. All sorts of posters from pop idols to Disney characters. *Open 09.30-20.00 Mon-Sat.*

Poster Shop   **4 F3**
28 James St WC2. 071-240 2526. A wonderful range of colourful posters. *Open 10.00-20.00 Mon-Sat, 12.00-19.00 Sun.*

★ *Sports* ★ ★ ★ ★ ★ ★ ★ ★ ★ ★ ★ ★ ★ ★ ★

ARCHERY

Quicks Archery Specialists
Hampton Court Rd, Hampton Court, Kingston, Surrey. 081-977 5790. Bows and arrows for the budding archer. *Open 09.30-13.00 & 14.15-17.00 Mon-Sat. Closed Wed.*

BOOKS

Sportspages   **4 E2**
94-96 Charing Cross Rd WC2. 071-240 9604. Sports bookshop covering all aspects of sport and fitness. Also stocks magazines and videos. *Open 09.30-19.00 Mon-Sat.*

BOXING

Lonsdale   **4 D3**
21 Beak St W1. 071-437 1526. All the greats of British boxing have bought clothes here at one time. Punch bags, mouth guards etc, plus boxing videos and books. *Open 09.00-18.00 Mon-Fri, to 17.00 Sat.*

CRICKET

For a good selection of equipment and clothing, try Hamleys or Lillywhites (see page 133).

FENCING

Leon Paul   **2 B5**
14 New North St WC1. 071-405 3832. All you need to be an expert fencer. *Open 09.00-17.00 Mon-Fri, 09.00-13.00 Sat.*

FISHING

Farlows of Pall Mall   **4 E4**
5 Pall Mall SW1. 071-839 2423. Game fishing tackle, shooting accessories and country clothing. *Open 09.00-18.00 Mon-Fri, to 16.00 Sat.*

Gerry's of Wimbledon
170 The Broadway SW19. 081-542 7792. General fishing tackle. *Open 09.00-17.30 Mon-Thur, to 18.00 Fri & Sat.*

House of Hardy 4 D4
61 Pall Mall SW1. 071-839 5515. Good selection of tackle and some of the finest hand-made rods in the world. *Open 09.00-18.00 Mon-Fri, to 16.00 Sat.*

FOOTBALL

Soccer Scene 4 D2
Carnaby Street W1. 071-437 1966. All the right boots, balls and shirts including exotic foreign strips. *Open 09.30-18.00 Mon-Sat, to 19.00 Thur.*

GENERAL

Hamleys 4 D3
188-196 Regent St W1. 071-734 3161. Sports clothes and equipment in the basement – you name it, they do it. *Open 10.00-18.00 Mon-Wed, to 20.00 Thur, to 18.30 Fri, 09.30-18.30 Sat.*

Lillywhites 4 E3
Lower Regent St SW1. 071-930 3181. Excellent collection of top English and Continental sports clothes and equipment. *Open 09.30-19.00 Mon-Fri, to 18.00 Sat.*

Olympus Sports 4 C2
301-309 Oxford St W1. 071-409 2619. Wide range of tennis, squash and badminton equipment, swimwear, skiwear; large training shoe department. Also luggage and sports bags. Other branches. *Open 09.30-18.00 Mon-Wed & Sat, to 20.00 Thur, to 19.00 Fri.*

Olympus Sports 4 C2
D.H. Evans, 318 Oxford St W1. 071-629 8800. The entire lower ground floor of the store is packed with clothes and equipment for tennis, squash, skiing, golf, riding, athletics, dance etc. *Open 10.00-18.30 Mon-Fri (to 20.00 Thur), to 19.00 Sat.*

ICE SKATING

Queens Ice Skating Shop 3 C3
Queens Ice Rink, Queensway W2. 071-229 4859. Everything you need to look like Torvill & Dean. *Open 11.00-12.30 & 14.30-16.30 Mon-Fri, 10.00-12.30 & 14.30-17.00 Sat & Sun.*

MARTIAL ARTS

Shaolin Way 4 E3
10 Little Newport St WC2. 071-734 6391. Martial arts equipment – judo suits, karate outfits, plus books and videos. *Open 11.00-19.00 Mon-Sun.*

RACKETS ▰▰▰▰▰▰▰▰▰▰▰▰▰▰▰▰▰▰▰▰

Racket Shop
22 Norland Rd W11. 071-603 0013. Good quality rackets for tennis, badminton and squash. *Open 10.00-18.00 Mon-Sat (to 13.00 Thur).*

RUNNING ▰▰▰▰▰▰▰▰▰▰▰▰▰▰▰▰▰▰▰▰

Run & Become, Become & Run   4 E6
42 Palmer St SW1. 071-222 1314. Specialist running shop. Vast range of running shoes plus footwear for many other sports. Also comprehensive stock of running clothes. Help and advice from running experts. *Open 09.00-18.00 Mon-Sat (to 20.00 Thur).*

Runners Need   1 D2
34 Parkway NW1. 071-267 7525. This small shop is stocked with shoes and clothing for all kinds of runners. Also a good information point on running events around London. *Open 10.00-18.00 Mon-Sat.*

SKATING ▰▰▰▰▰▰▰▰▰▰▰▰▰▰▰▰▰▰▰▰

Skate Attack
95 Highgate Rd NW5. 071-267 6961. Sells and hires roller skates, ice skates and skateboards. *Open 10.00-18.00 Mon-Fri, 09.00-18.00 Sat.*

SKIING ▰▰▰▰▰▰▰▰▰▰▰▰▰▰▰▰▰▰▰▰

Alpine Sports   3 B6
215 Kensington High St W8. 071-938 1911. All the equipment you need for the slopes. *Open 10.00-19.00 Mon-Fri (to 20.00 Thur), 09.00-18.00 Sat, 11.00-17.00 Sun.*

C & A   4 B3
501-509 Oxford St W1. 071-629 7272. Sports World section has a good, colourful range of skiwear for toddlers upwards. Other branches. *Open 09.30-19.00 Mon-Fri (to 20.00 Thur), 09.00-19.00 Sat.*

Snow & Rock   3 B6
188 Kensington High St W8. 071-937 0872. Walking and climbing gear for summer; the latest in ski outfits for winter. *Open 10.00-19.00 Mon-Fri, 09.00-18.00 Sat; (Dec-Easter) 11.00-17.00 Sun.*

WATERSPORTS ▰▰▰▰▰▰▰▰▰▰▰▰▰▰▰▰▰▰

Ocean Leisure   4 F4
Embankment Place, 11-14 Northumberland Ave WC2. 071-930 5050. Biggest watersports outlet in the country with diving, sailing and waterskiing equipment, a chandlery, underwater photography, charts and books. Diving courses

for over 14s. *Open 09.30-17.30 Mon-Fri, to 19.00 Thur, to 18.00 Sat.*
Windsurfer's World
146 Chiswick High Rd W4. 081-994 6769. All the newest and the best for the windsurfer. *Open 09.30-18.00 Mon-Sat (to 20.00 Thur).*
Yacht Parts
99 Fulham Palace Rd W6. 081-741 9803. Yacht equipment, clothing, books. *Open 09.00-17.30 Mon-Fri, to 17.00 Sat.*

★ *Stamps* ★ ★ ★ ★ ★ ★ ★ ★ ★ ★ ★ ★ ★ ★

O J Hill   **4 F3**
79 Strand WC2. 071-836 2579. First day covers, foreign issues. *Open 10.00-17.00 Mon-Fri, to 14.00 Sat.*
Stanley Gibbons   **4 F3**
399 Strand WC2. 071-836 8444. Sets of commemorative stamps; special mail box for first day issue stamping. *Open 08.30-18.00 Mon-Fri, 10.00-16.00 Sat.*

★ *Theme Shops* ★ ★ ★ ★ ★ ★ ★ ★ ★ ★ ★

The Disney Store   **4 D3**
140 Regent St W1. 071-287 6558. Huge range of Disney products; videos, books, toys, stationery, clothing, jewellery, homeware. *Open 09.30-19.00 Mon-Sat, to 20.00 Thur, 12.00-18.00 Sun.*
Sherlock Holmes Memorabilia Company   **1 B5**
230 Baker St NW1. 071-486 1426. The only shop in the world exclusively selling Sherlock Holmes related objects – mugs, T-shirts, posters, postcards, antique books and period magazines. *Open 09.30-17.30 Mon-Sat, 10.00-14.00 Sun.*
Tin Tin Shop   **4 F3**
34 Floral St WC2. 071-836 1131. Packed with all Hergé's books about the young hero, plus T-shirts, posters and other novelties. *Open 10.00-18.00 Mon-Sat, 12.00-17.00 Sun.*
Warner Brothers Studio Store
The Bentall Centre, Kingston-upon-Thames. 081-974 8893. Warner Brothers movie memorabilia including T-shirts, toys, cartoon art, videos and books. Regent Street store due to open at the end of 1994.

★ *Toys & Games* ★ ★ ★ ★ ★ ★ ★ ★ ★ ★ ★

Many department stores have very good toy departments, especially Harrods, Selfridges and Heal's. Most of the following specialist shops will send catalogues on request. The British Toy and Hobby Manufacturers' Association, 80

Camberwell Rd SE5 will put you in touch with the manufac-
turer if you have a problem or query concerning a toy.
Remember you can always borrow toys – phone or send an
sae to Play Matters, The National Association of Toy and
Leisure Libraries, 68 Churchway NW1 (071-387 9592) for
details of your local toy library.

Children's World

317 Cricklewood Bdwy NW2. 081-208 1088. Children go
down a helter-skelter to enter this shop which sells toys,
accessories and clothes. Café serving cheap snacks. Mother
and baby room. *Open 10.00-20.00 Mon-Fri, 09.00-18.00 Sat,
10.00-17.00 Sun.*

Doll's House　　　　　　　　　　　　　　　　　　　　**4 F3**

29 Covent Garden Market WC2. 071-379 7243. Wide
range of beautiful, hand-made dolls' houses and miniature

Markets

There are dozens of markets in London; they are always
hectic and colourful. Even if you don't buy anything it is
worth going along for the atmosphere. People have been
trading in the streets since the city's earliest beginnings and
some of the markets have been held for hundreds of years.
But remember that on wet days and *Mondays* markets tend
to be rather lifeless.

There are two sorts of markets; wholesale, which sell
goods to other tradespeople and shopkeepers, and retail,
which sell to the general public.

Berwick Street　　　　　　　　　　　　　　　　　　**4 D2**

Soho W1. Busy general market in the heart of Soho; the
fruit and vegetables are good and always beautifully stacked
on the stalls. Also meat, and excellent cheese, fresh fish
and household goods. *Open 09.00-18.00 Mon-Sat.*

Billingsgate (Wholesale)

North Quay, West India Docks Rd, Isle of Dogs E14. The
new site of London's principal fish market, moved from its
old location in the City. Tons of fish are handled at this market each week which has been in operation since Saxon
times. Some of the porters still wear 'bobbing' hats made of
thick leather and wood with flat tops for carrying boxes.
Open 05.00-08.00 Mon-Sat.

Camden Lock　　　　　　　　　　　　　　　　　　　**1 D1**

Where Chalk Farm Rd crosses the Regent's Canal NW1.
Amongst the cobbled courtyards and warehouses of the
lock is a huge expanse of market selling everything from
antique clothing to pine furniture. A number of interesting
food stalls. *Open 09.00-18.00 Sat & Sun.*

furniture in traditional styles for children as well as collectors. Some of the houses and furniture come in kit form so you can assemble your own. *Open 10.00-20.00 Mon-Sat.*

Dolls' Hospital
16 Dawes Rd SW6. 071-385 2081. Casualty department for broken limbs, spare part surgery, antique restoration etc. Also a few toys and dolls for sale. *Phone for opening times.*

Early Learning Centre   **3 B6**
225 Kensington High St W8. 071-937 0419. Bright, durable, educational toys for babies upwards. A wonderful selection of jack-in-the-boxes. Under 8s can try out the toys in the play area. Other branches. *Open 09.00-18.00 Mon-Sat.*

Eric Snook's Toyshop   **4 F3**
32 The Market, Covent Garden WC2. 071-379 7681. Smart

Covent Garden Market   **4 F3**
The Piazza WC2. Until 1974, this was the site of London's principal wholesale fruit and vegetable market. Now the central piazza and streets radiating from it are full of charming stalls and interesting shops. The main market, known as the Apple Market, is in the piazza. On *Mondays* there's an antique market, whilst during the rest of the week the stalls are full of original high-class imaginative crafts, clothing and jewellery. Street shows and cafés abound.

New Covent Garden (Wholesale)   **7 D5**
Nine Elms SW8. London's foremost wholesale fruit, vegetable and flower market which has been in its present location since the end of 1974, when it was moved from its central location (see above). Extremely lively and colourful and worth a visit if you can get up in time. *Open from 04.00 Mon-Sun.* Flower market in *summer*. Admission charge.

Petticoat Lane   **5 F1**
Radiates from Middlesex St E1. Huge bustling complex selling everything under the sun. This is real East End territory. Streets leading off the main market specialise in different things. Petticoat Lane got its name in the 1600s when clothes sellers congregated there. *Open 09.00-14.00 Sun.*

Portobello Market   **3 A2**
Portobello Rd W11. The first dealers here were gypsies buying and selling horses and herbs. Now there is a much wider range of goods. The market stretches for the entire length of Portobello Road and has an enormous amount of second-hand junk and bric-à-brac. There's also a good selection of fruit and vegetables during the week.

toyshop selling Beatrix Potter characters and hand-made wooden toys. *Open 10.00-19.00 Mon-Sat, 11.00-18.00 Sun.*

Hamleys 4 D3

188-196 Regent St W1. 071-734 3161. Largest toy shop in London – six floors of it. Has nearly every toy and game you can think of. All ages. Children can try out the toys in play areas. *Open 10.00-18.00 Mon-Wed, to 20.00 Thur, to 18.30 Fri, 09.30-18.30 Sat.*

Just Games 4 D3

71 Brewer St W1. 071-734 6124. Has all the old favourites, such as Scrabble, chess and backgammon, plus some more unusual games. *Open 10.00-18.00 Mon-Sat (to 19.00 Thur).*

Kristin Baybars

7 Mansfield Rd NW3. 071-267 0934. Tiny treasure chest which specialises in craftsman-made dolls' houses, miniatures and unusual toys. *Open 11.15-18.00 Tue-Sat. Phone for appointment to visit out-of-hours.*

Pollock's Museum & Toy Shop 4 D1

1 Scala St W1. 071-636 3452. Fascinating small shop which sells toys, old-fashioned and modern, and the famous Victorian cut-out model theatres. Also sells toys from other parts of the world. *Open 10.00-17.00 Mon-Sat.*

Benjamin Pollock's Toy Shop 4 F3

44 Covent Garden Market WC2. 071-379 7866. Sells toys and Victorian cut-out model theatres for children and collectors. *Open 10.30-18.00 Mon-Sat.*

Singing Tree

69 New King's Rd SW6. 071-736 4527. Not just for children, this amazing shop stocks new and antique dolls' houses and everything imaginable to go in them. Collector's items in miniature. Mail-order service. *Open 10.00-17.30 Mon-Sat.*

Toys 'R' Us

Tilling Rd, Brent Cross NW2. 081-209 0019. Huge toy warehouse selling games and toys for children of all ages. *Open 09.00-20.00 Mon-Sat, to 21.00 Thur, 10.00-18.00 Sun.*

Virgin Games Centre 4 D2

100 Oxford St W1. 071-637 7911. Renowned for its incredible fantasy games. Virgin even have a whole department given over to war games. Stock the complete Trivial Pursuit range and a floor of computer games. *Open 09.30-19.00 Mon-Sat, to 20.00 Thur.*

★ Party Time

★ Entertainment ★ ★ ★ ★ ★ ★ ★ ★ ★ ★ ★ ★

Carolyn's Puppets
12 York Rd, Richmond, Surrey. 081-940 8407. A traditional puppet show for children of 2-8 years, with rod puppets, magic, games and fairy stories. Also costume shows for 6-10 year-olds in which the children participate.

Frog Hollow
15 Victoria Grove, Kensington W8. 071-581 5493. Has a list of recommended entertainers. *Open 09.00-17.30 Mon-Sat.*

Juke Box Junction
12 Toneborough, Abbey Rd NW8. 071-328 6206. The place to go to hire, or even buy, a juke box. Over 3000 rock 'n' rolling tunes to get a party going. *Open 10.30-18.00 Mon-Fri, 11.00-16.00 Sat.*

Len Belmont
48 Morland Estate E8. 071-254 8300. Well-known and popular children's entertainer with ventriloquist, magic and balloon modelling acts. Guaranteed to get a party started.

"Prof" Alexander's Punch & Judy
59 Wilton Way E8. 071-254 0416. Traditional show. He has performed at the Albert Hall, the National Theatre and the Polka Children's Theatre. Also does magic shows.

Simon Lee Discos
15 Malcolm Rd, Coulsdon, Surrey. 081-668 7592. Simon provides a mixture of music, competitions, party games and disco entertainment for children of all ages. Mainly works in SE London.

Tiddleywinks
66 Hurlingham Court, Ranelagh Gdns SW6. 071-736 1842. Run by actress Gabrielle Lister, this is a combination of theatre, dance and drama, usually with lots of audience participation. Gabrielle will provide costumes and make-up and the children can perform for their parents at the end of the party. Also story-telling sessions.

William Bartholomew   6 B6
18 Talina Centre, Bagleys Lane SW6. 071-731 8328. Has been running discotheques for 15 years and provides excellent entertainment for children's parties. Lots of special effects and a party organising service.

★ *Novelties & Costumes* ★ ★ ★ ★ ★ ★ ★

Barnum's
67 Hammersmith Rd W14. 071-602 1211. Piles of masks, balloons, flags and party kits for your next party. *Open 09.00-18.00 Mon-Fri, 10.00-17.00 Sat.*

Carnival Store
95 Hammersmith Rd W14. 071-603 7824. Amazing variety of costumes for hire, for every occasion. *Open 10.00-13.00 & 14.30-18.00 Mon-Fri, 10.00-13.00 Sat.*

Circus Circus
176 Wandsworth Bridge Rd SW6. 071-731 4128. Party shop providing a complete party service. Sells all the party paraphernalia. Can supply entertainers and cakes and organise theme parties. Hire section includes everything from tables and chairs to bouncy castles. *Open 09.30-18.30 Mon-Sat, 10.00-17.00 Sun.*

City Dress Arcade
437 Bethnal Green Rd E2. 071-739 2645. Costume hire at a very reasonable price. *Open 10.30-16.30 Mon-Sat. Closed Thur.*

Escapade   1 E2
150 Camden High St NW1. 071-485 7384. Get all your party kit here. Stuffed full of costumes, tricks, masks, wigs, jokes and novelties. *Open 10.00-19.00 Mon-Fri, to 18.00 Sat.*

Frog Hollow
15 Victoria Grove, Kensington W8. 071-581 5493. Fun and

wacky. Specialise in children's party goods – presents, toys and paper tableware plus helium balloons. Children's costumes for sale. Also hire out low tables and chairs. *Open 09.00-17.30 Mon-Sat.*

Hamleys   **4 D3**

188-196 Regent St W1. 071-734 3161. Sells a large selection of costumes and masks for 2-10 year-olds. *Open 10.00-18.00 Mon-Wed, to 20.00 Thur, to 18.30 Fri, 09.30-18.30 Sat.*

Just Balloons   **7 C2**

127 Wilton Rd SW1. 071-434 3039. Any type of balloons – rubber, metallic and even specially printed ones with your own message or design. *Open 09.30-18.00 Mon-Sat.*

Non Stop Party Shop

694 Fulham Rd SW6. 071-384 1491. Everything from low price whistles to the more expensive party accessory available here. Other branch: Kensington High Street W8. *Open 09.30-18.00 Mon-Sat.*

Theatre Zoo   **4 F2**

21 Earlham St WC2. 071-836 3150. Definitely the place to go for fancy dress. Animal costumes for hire, grotesque and unusual face masks, false feet, hats, hands, wigs, moustaches and stage make-up. They do not have a showroom so it is advisable to phone in advance to discuss what you're looking for. *Open 09.00-17.30 Mon-Fri.*

★ *Organisers* ★ ★ ★ ★ ★ ★ ★ ★ ★ ★ ★ ★

AM PM Catering   **7 B6**

15-17 Ingate Place SW8. 071-622 6229. Will organise the whole party, including entertainment. Catering is done to your budget. Various venues.

Annie Fryer Catering   **6 C5**

134 Lots Rd SW10. 071-351 4333. Organises theme parties for small children and teenagers. Menus designed to the children's taste. Can also provide entertainment such as magicians, game organisers and venues for the party. Homemade birthday cakes to any theme or design.

Hamlins   **3 B6**

3 Abingdon Rd W8. 071-937 3442. Caters at home. Can arrange hire of tables, chairs, entertainers etc. Traditional party food and novelty birthday cakes. Food includes sandwiches, jellies, ice-cream, animal-shaped cakes.

Entertaining à la Claire
46 Quinton St SW18. 081-946 8490. Claire can organise children's parties right down to the entertainment and the novelty cake.

Norman Myers
80 Bridge Lane NW11. 081-458 4295. Norman is widely known and very experienced in children's entertainment. He will take care of everything, leaving you and the children to sit back, relax and enjoy a traditional party. Catering, magic, balloons, films, Punch & Judy shows, puppets, games and prizes are all provided.

Party Professionals
33 Kensington Park Rd W11. 071-221 3438. Organises straightforward parties in the home, or extravaganzas such as a circus in a tent.

★ *Venues* ★ ★ ★ ★ ★ ★ ★ ★ ★ ★ ★ ★ ★ ★

Gurnell Pool
Ruislip Road East W13. 081-998 3241. Private use of the baby pool or shallow pool for *2 hours*. Complete with life-

guard, inflatables and tables and chairs for tea (bring your own food). Book three months in advance.

Madame Tussaud's   1 C5

Marylebone Rd NW1. 071-935 6861. Parties of up to 20 children can be held in the Pier Café. Old-fashioned slot machines and a shooting gallery, with Benny Hill looking on. Hamburger-style food.

McDonald's

Hold parties providing a hamburger meal, games, hats and balloons. Party pack for the birthday girl or boy. Facilities differ at each restaurant. *Phone your local branch for details.*

Orangery   3 A5

Holland Park W8. 071-602 7344. This conservatory was once the ballroom of Holland House. Holds a maximum of 50 seated. You can bring your own food or use its caterers (but no outside caterers).

Polka Children's Theatre

240 The Broadway SW19. 081-543 4888/0363. You can book a party in the pantry at any time without actually watching the show. The room holds a maximum of 60 children but you must book in advance.

Quasar Centre

Frobisher Rd N8. 081-348 9798. The Quasar Space Game is a technological version of hide and seek with laser beams. Hire the centre for a 45-minute game (maximum 24 children) followed by tea in the viewing gallery. You can bring your own food or they will organise for pizzas to be delivered. Plus a Quasar T-shirt for the birthday boy or girl.

Rose Garden   1 C4

Regent's Park NW1. 071-935 5729. A good place to book for children's parties. Special party food, with soft drinks, cakes, sweets, crisps and balloons. Active entertainments available such as face painting and bouncy castle. Entertainer available on request.

★ Holidays

★ *Holiday Organisations* ★ ★ ★ ★ ★ ★ ★

There are innumerable organisations which arrange holidays and special interest camps for unaccompanied children, and others which deal in family holidays. Check out some of the ones below to get some ideas:

Ardmore Adventure
11-15 High St, Marlow, Bucks. (0628) 890060. Adventure holidays in areas around London – Henley, Chalfont St Giles, Crowthorne, Maidenhead and Aylesbury. The camps are held during the *summer holidays*. There are all sorts of activities to take part in including archery, volleyball, swimming (at some centres), air-rifle shooting, performing arts, baseball, basketball, canoeing, plus arts and crafts. Also have organised activities such as face painting and field games.

Camp Beaumont
Bridge House, Orchard Lane, Huntingdon, Cambs. (0480) 456123. Residential and day camps around London – Brentwood, Mill Hill, Windsor and Wimbledon – *during the summer*. An incredible range of activities to get involved in – water sports, ball sports, motor sports, stage and screen. Centres vary in the activities they offer so everyone is matched to a suitable centre. From nursery day camps for the small ones to holidays for the independent teenager.

John Ridgway School of Adventure
Ardmore, Rhiconich, by Lairg, Sutherland. (0971) 521229. International *summer school* for 12 plus. Outdoor adventure holiday with off-shore and dinghy sailing, hill walking, rock climbing, canoeing and survival courses in remote Highland coastal areas. Accommodation in chalet buildings on the shores of a remote sea loch.

Ocean Youth Club
Bus Station, South St, Gosport, Hants PO12 1EP. (0705) 528421. Cruising courses for a weekend, one week or longer, covers basic seamanship. 12-24 year-olds can learn

aboard ocean-going yachts based at different ports around the country. Longer cruises quite often reach foreign shores. The boats are big enough to cross oceans, but small enough for everyone to have a part in sailing them. Beginners welcome.

PGL Young Adventure
Alton Court, Penyard Lane, Ross-on-Wye, Herefordshire. (0989) 764211. Holidays for ages 6-18, and family adventure holidays. Up to 40 activities including canoeing, pony trekking, sailing, camping and hobby holidays under expert guidance at 30 locations in Britain and abroad. Brochures available.

STA Schooners
2a The Hard, Portsmouth, Hants. (0705) 832055. Sail Training Association adventure sailing courses take place in the schooners *Sir Winston Churchill* and *Malcolm Miller* from *Mar-Nov*. They aim to develop strength of character in teenagers by encouraging participants to crew ships as members of a team. No previous experience required.

Suzanne's Riding School
Copse Farm, Brookshill Drive, Harrow Weald, Middx. 081-954 3618. A school with 70 horses set in 135 hectares (300 acres) of farmland. Regular 'Own-a-Pony' weeks in *summer* where you are allocated a pony to look after and ride for a week.

Trent Park Equestrian Centre
Bramley Rd, Southgate N14. 081-363 8630/9005. 'Own-a-Pony' weeks where everyone 'adopts' a pony and visits the stable every day for a week to look after and ride it. Also 4-day holidays looking after a pony and riding it twice a day. *Phone for details.*

YHA Adventure Holidays
Youth Hostel Association, Trevelyan House, St Stephen's Hill, St Albans, Herts. (0727) 55215. Adventure holidays for 11-15 year-olds (in groups of 10-12) with experienced instructors. Large range of special interest holidays as well as multi-activity holidays. Older YHA members can also arrange their own cycling or walking holidays and make use of the YHA hostels.

EXCHANGES

Amitié Internationale des Jeunes
36 Chaulden House Gdns, Hemel Hempsted, Herts. (0442) 250886. Exchanges between French and British, 11-18 year-

olds. Escorts are provided on the journey between London and Paris.

Central Bureau for Educational 4 B2
Visits & Exchanges
Seymour Mews House, Seymour Mews W1. 071-486 5101. They publish several excellent guides including *Volunteer Work*, *Working Holidays*, *A Year Between*, *Study Holidays*, *Teach Abroad* and *Home from Home*, covering opportunities both here and abroad. Send an sae (no personal callers).

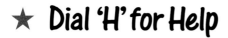

★ Dial 'H' for Help

If you are in trouble and need help, do not keep it to yourself. There are a number of organisations which can offer advice and help for parents and children. We have listed some of them here, plus some other organisations it may be helpful to know about.

ANOREXIA

Eating Disorders Association
Sackville Place, Magdalen St, Norwich. (0603) 621414 *09.00-16.00 Mon-Fri.* Youth line (0603) 765050 *16.00-18.00 Mon-Wed.*
Anorexics Anonymous
24 Westmoreland Rd SW13. 081-748 3994.

BABY-SITTING

Baby-sitters Unlimited
2 Napoleon Rd, Twickenham, Middx. 081-892 8888. Annual membership and fee at each booking. Hourly rates vary according to the time of day. Covers central London.
Childminders   1 C6
9 Paddington St W1. 071-935 9763/2049. Annual membership and fee at each booking. Hourly rates. Covers 20-mile radius from central London.
Universal Aunts
PO Box 304, Clapham SW4. 071-738 8937. A well-known agency that will provide all kinds of domestic help, including baby-sitting. Office *open Mon-Fri 09.30-17.00.*

COUNSELLING

National Youth Agency
17-23 Albion St, Leicester LE1. (0533) 471200.

DESPERATE

Childline
Freepost 1111, London N1 0BR. 0800 1111. A freephone number. Will listen, advise and, where necessary, act to prevent children being abused.
Samaritans
Look in your phone book for the number. They listen to and

support anyone of any age, about anything. No worry, no anxiety, no feeling is too trivial, and they won't tell anyone.

DISABLED IN LONDON

Artsline   1 F3
54 Chalton St NW1. 071-388 2227. Artsline is an advice and information service on the arts in the Greater London area for people with disabilities. It can give details of places, events and activities and their accessibility to people who may have difficulties.

DRUG ABUSE

Standing Conference on Drug Abuse   5 C5
(SCODA), Waterbridge House, 32-33 Loman St SE1. 071-928 9500.

EDUCATION

Advisory Centre for Education
Unit 1b, Aberdeen Studios, 22-24 Highbury Grove N5. 071-354 8321. Provides free help and advice for parents, students and teachers. Ask for their list of publications. They also publish information sheets and an excellent magazine, *ACE Bulletin*, available by annual subscription. Manned *14.00-17.00 Mon-Fri*.

Gabbitas Educational Consultants   4 D3
6-8 Sackville St W1. 071-734 0161. Expert advice on the choice of independent schools and colleges, higher education and careers.

Independent Schools Information Service   4 D6
(ISIS), 56 Buckingham Gate SW1. 071-630 8793 (Head Office). Information about independent and private schools.

EMERGENCIES

Dial 999 from any phone box (no money is needed) and ask for fire, police or ambulance.

HOSPITAL

Action for Sick Children   1 G4
Argyle House, 29-31 Euston Rd NW1. 071-833 2041. Gives advice and information to parents and carers of sick children.

INFORMATION

Kidsline
071-222 8070. For information on children's classes, clubs, events, sports and entertainments. *Open 16.00-18.00 Mon-Fri in term time, 09.00-16.00 Mon-Fri in school hols.*

JOBS

From the age of 13 you can do two hours part-time work on school days, eight hours on *Sat* and one hour's work on *Sun*. Your local authority may have regulations about places and conditions.

LEGAL RIGHTS

Children's Legal Centre
20 Compton Terrace N1. 071-359 6251. Advice line *14.00-17.00.*
National Council for Civil Liberties   5 E5
21 Tabard St SE1. 071-403 3888.

LOST SOMETHING

BR (all regions but Southern). Property is held at the station where it was handed in. After about a week, it's forwarded to Central Lost Property, Marylebone Station, Marylebone Rd NW1. 071-387 9400. For Southern Region apply to the local railway station.
London Transport: call in person or write to London Transport Lost Property, 200 Baker St W1 (**1 B5**). *Open 09.30-14.00 Mon-Fri.*
Taxis: apply to 15 Penton St N1 (**2 C3**) 071-833 0996. Alternatively, apply to the nearest police station.

ONE PARENT FAMILIES

Gingerbread   4 G3
35 Wellington St WC2. 071-240 0953. Acts as a central information service for a national network of independent self-help groups. They organise *after school and holiday* activities for school-aged children with a working parent.

National Council for One Parent Families
255 Kentish Town Rd NW5. 071-267 1361.

ORGANISATIONS

Barnardo's
Tanner's Lane, Barkingside, Ilford, Essex. 081-550 8822. Provides homes for children as well as trying to prevent the breaking up of family life.

Child Poverty Action Group   2 F4
1-5 Bath St EC1. 071-253 3406. More a pressure group than a charity, but they do advise on obtaining social security etc.

Invalid Children's Aid Nationwide   2 E5
Barbican City Gate, 1-3 Dufferin St EC1. 071-253 9111. Special schools for asthmatic and non-communicating children.

National Association for Gifted Children
Park Campus, Boughton Green Rd, Northampton. (0604) 792300. Advice of all kinds for parents and teachers of gifted children. Activities for the children. Newsletter *four times a year.*

National Association for Mental Health
(MIND), Granta House, 15-19 Broadway, Stratford E15. 081-519 2122. Branches throughout the UK. Gives help and advice on mind, body and emotional problems for people of all ages.

National Society for Autistic Children
276 Willesden Lane NW2. 081-451 1114. Advice and help. Special schools. Playgroup.

Royal Society for Mentally Handicapped Children   2 E5
and Adults
123 Golden Lane EC1. 071-454 0454. Works with people with learning disabilities, their parents and carers. Care centre, day nurseries, leisure clubs, training schemes, residential houses.

National Society for the Prevention of   2 G5
Cruelty to Children
NSPCC National Centre, 42 Curtain Road EC2. 071-825 2500. Offers help and advice in times of stress or crises

affecting children. Investigates reports of ill-treatment. 'Battered child' research department.

POLICE

New Scotland Yard have a public relations department which you can contact with reference to any problems you may be experiencing that involves the police.

National Council for Civil Liberties   **5 E5**
21 Tabard St SE1. 071-403 3888. Issues leaflets on your rights about arrest, questioning, being searched in the street, the police station, bail, complaints against the police, search of premises, seizure of property and legal costs.

RAPE

Rape Crisis Centre
071-837 1600. Emergency number manned *10.00-23.00 Mon-Fri, 09.00-24.00 Sat & Sun.* Or write to PO Box 69, London WC1.

RUNAWAYS

Message Home
0800 919616. A *24-hr* phone service which will pass on messages without revealing your whereabouts.

Missing Persons
081-392 2000. A *24-hr* phone service that offers practical advice and support.

Piccadilly Advisory Centre   **4 E3**
100 Shaftesbury Ave W1. 071-434 3773. Free nightline on 0800 446441.

★ Index

NICHOLSON

MAPS

**KEY TO
MAP
PAGES**

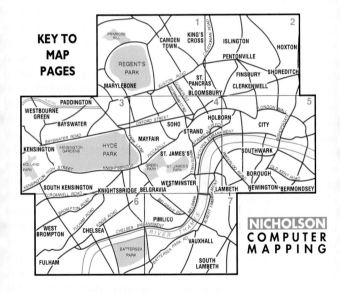

NICHOLSON
**COMPUTER
MAPPING**

SHOPS 071-

Aquascutum 734 6090
Army & Navy 834 1234
Asprey 493 6767
Austin Reed 734 6789
BHS (Kensington High St) 937 0919
BHS (Oxford St) 629 2011
Barkers 937 5432
C & A 629 7272
Cartier 493 6962
Christie's 839 9060
Conran Shop 589 7401
DH Evans 626 8800
Debenhams 580 3000
Dickins & Jones 734 7070
Dillons 636 1577
Fenwick 629 9161
Fortnum & Mason 734 8040
Foyles 437 5660
General Trading Company 730 0411
Habitat (King's Rd) 351 1211
Habitat (Tottenham Court Rd) 631 3880
Hamleys 734 3161
Harrods 730 1234
Harvey Nichols 235 5000
Hatchards 439 9921
Heal's 636 1666
HMV 631 3423
Jaeger 734 8211
John Lewis 629 7711
Laura Ashley 437 9760
Liberty 734 1234
Lillywhites 930 3181
Littlewoods 434 4301
London Pavilion 437 1838
Maples 387 7000
Marks & Spencer (Ken. High St) 938 3711
Marks & Spencer (Marble Arch) 935 7954
Marks & Spencer (Oxford St) 437 7722
Mothercare 629 6621
Next (Kensington High St) 938 4211
Next (Regent St) 434 2515
Peter Jones 730 3434
Selfridges 629 1234
Simpson 734 2002
Sotheby's 493 8080
Top Shop 636 7700
Tower Records 439 2500
Trocadero 439 1791
Victoria Place Shopping Centre 931 8811
Virgin Megastore 631 1234
Whiteleys Shopping Centre 229 8844

© Nicholson

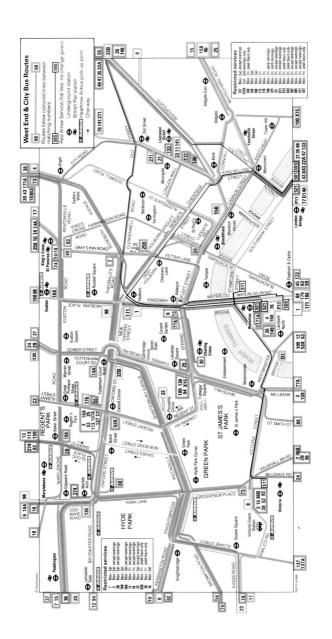

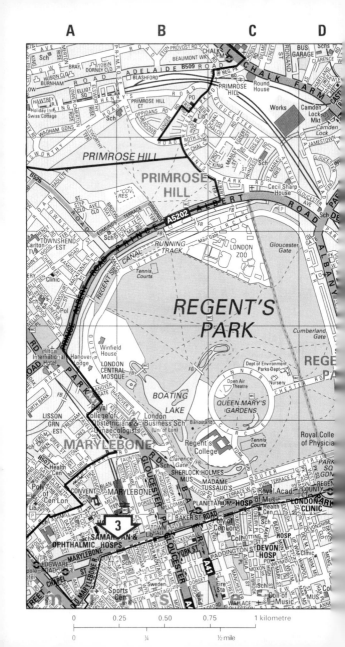

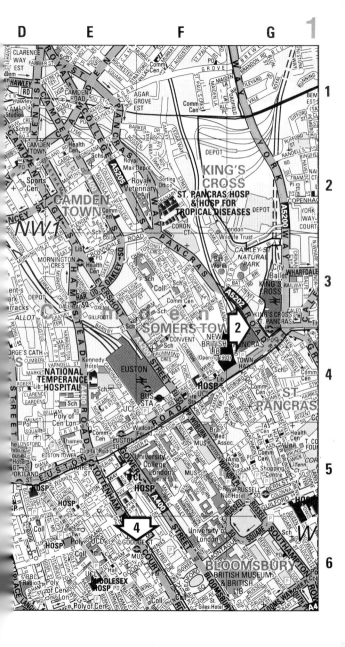

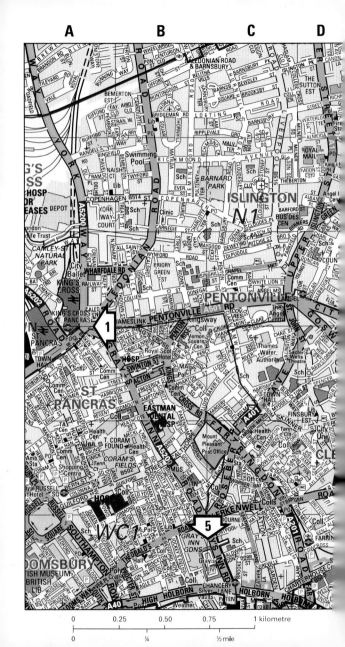

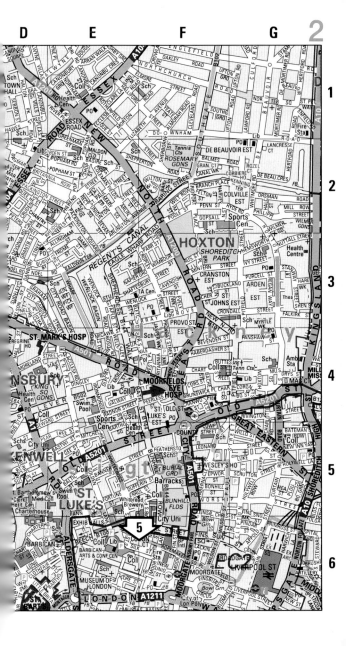

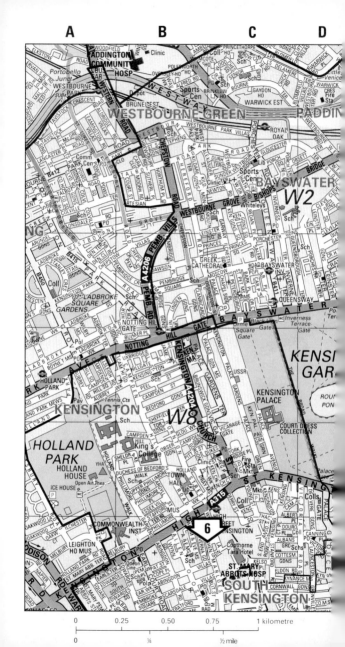

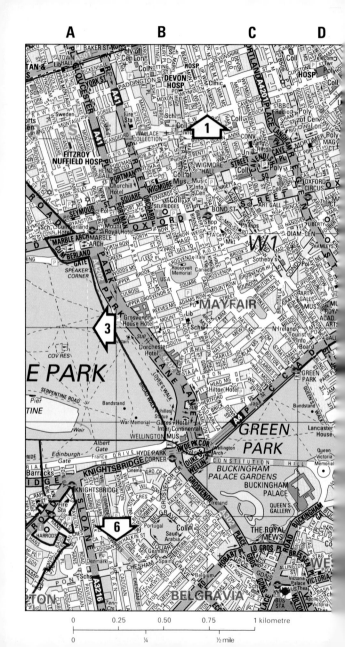

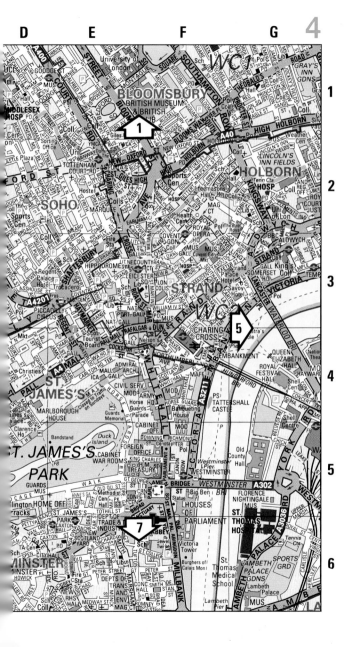

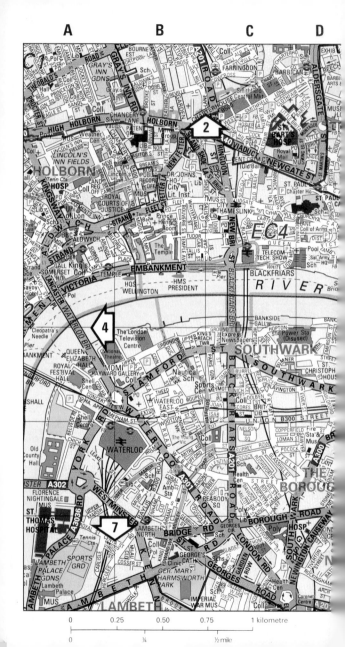

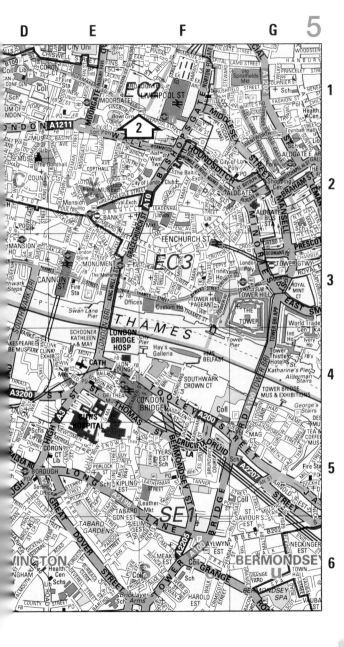

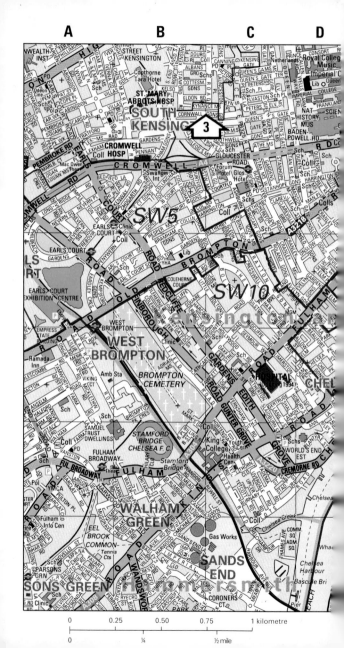

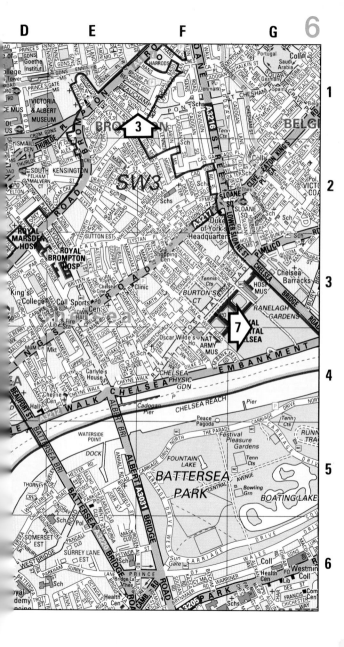

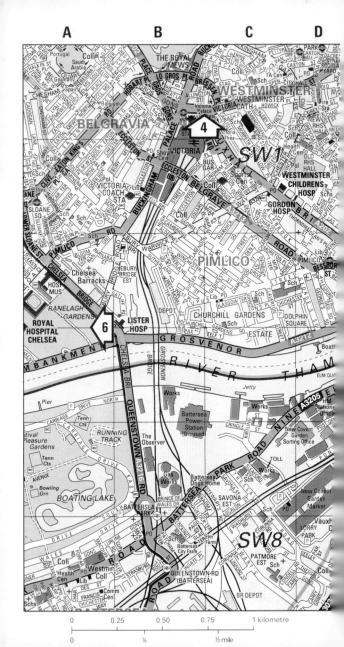

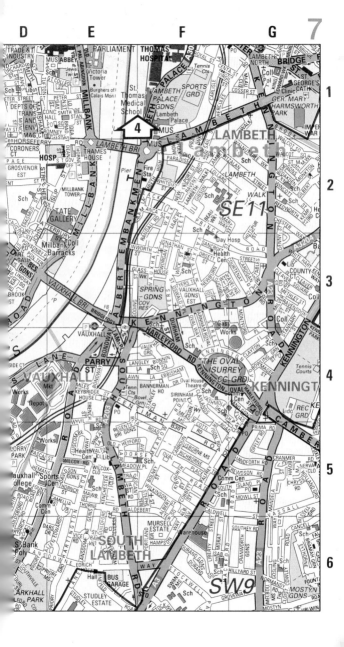

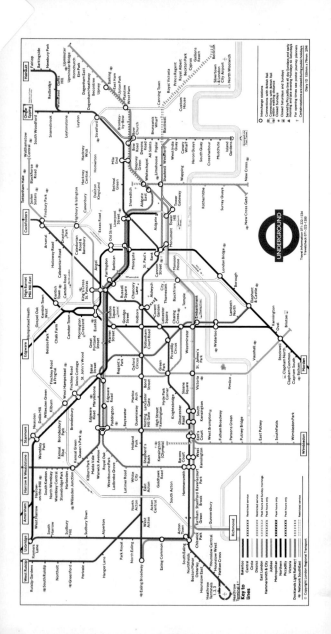